The Big Huge Bk of Mc

Also by E.J. Stewart

Changes
The War of Mirrors
The Lyre Birds
The Wayfaring Dolphin
The Bow of Burning Gold
Listening Skills for the 21st Century
Simulator
Simulator LIGHT
Simulator MEDIUM
Simulator JUNIOR
Inklings
Inklings II
Interview-Outerview
Planet of the Apps
The Seneschals of Dol

The Big Huge Bk of Mc

A Longer History of the (Mc)Donald Clan

Jan Eylander Jackson Stewart

Leaf & Vine Books

San Francisco

© 2022 by Leaf & Vine Books

All rights reserved. No part of this publication may be reproduced, stored in a retrieval system, or transmitted, in any form or by any means, electronic, mechanical, photocopying, recording, or otherwise, without the prior written permission of the publisher.

Published by Leaf & Vine Books
387 Ivy Street
San Francisco, CA 94102

ISBN: 978-0-9786087-6-7

Printed in the United States of America.

for
Annabelle Grace Taylor
Alaina Katherine Taylor
Christopher Wren Stewart
Percival Constantine Stewart
etc.

Contents

Part 1 The Hebrews
   Table 1: Descendants of Adam and Eve
     From Shem to Darda
     From Ham to Priam
   Table 2: Descendants of Noah, featuring Ham
     From Japheth to Miles
     Two Scotas

Part 2 Troy
   Table 3: The Mythological Kings
     From Darda to Thor
   Table 4: Callirhoe's Ancestors

Part 3 The Scandinavians
     From Odin to Ragnar Lothbrok
     Saint Osgyth

Part 4 Vikings in Ireland
     From Ivar B. to Prince Ivar of Waterford
   Table 5: The Ancestors of Slani ingen Brian
     From Ivar II to Gillebride
     The Battle of Stamford Bridge

Part 5 Ireland
     From Heremon to Eogan Find mac Neill
     Saint Patrick

Part 6 The Kings of Argyll
     Argyle, Dal Riada, The Lords of the Isles,
     The Picts
   Table 6: Kings of Argyll + Kings of Scotland
     From Earca nic Loarn to Fergus Mor
     From King Alpin to Duncan I
   Table 7: Huntingdon / Bruce / Stewart
     From Malcolm III to Marjorie Bruce
   Table 8: The Donalds
     From Somerled to John Mor Tanister
     The Campbells and the McDonalds
     From Donald Balloch to Sir Daniel MacD.
     The Battle of Bloody Bay
     The Fairy Flag of the MacLeods
     The Eigg Massacre
   Table 9: O'Neill / O'Cahan
     The Glencoe Massacre

Part 7 The Americans
     The Siege of Derry
   Table 10: The Americans
     From Sir John MacDonnell to Jan Stewart

A Few Notable Mc's

Essay: The Triumvirate, or, The Laws of
     Nova Dalriada

Appendix 1 – The Big Huge Bk of Mc
Appendix 2 – The Hebrews
Appendix 3 – The Trojans
Appendix 4 – The Scythians
Appendix 5 – The Scandinavians
Appendix 6 – The Lineage of Queen Tea Tephi
Appendix 7 – The Irish
Appendix 8 – The Kings of Ireland / Scotland
Appendix 9 – The Donalds / McDonalds

Foreword

This volume is dedicated to my parents Jack and Faye who, during their golden years, traveled about the country visiting relatives (both dead and alive), in an effort to reconstruct their past. Given the tools that they had available at that time, their efforts yielded impressive dividends. In a previous volume called *The Seneschals of Dol*, I expounded on those efforts, focusing mainly on my paternal ancestors. Yet as I delved deeper into those people's lives, I became intrigued by the possibilities that the ancestries of their *wives* might offer.

One person in particular seemed to hold the key to further investigations, and that is my father's great-grandmother, Rebecca McDonald (his mother's grandmother). Through this woman we can trace the history of the McDonalds all the way back through time to King Ivar II of Waterford, Ireland, and beyond. Along the way, it behooves us to stop for a moment and examine the personage of John MacDonald, Lord of the Isles, who was born in 1318. His wife was Margaret Stewart, whose lineage goes back (via Marjorie Bruce) through the Kings of Scotland, the Kings of Argyll, and the Kings of Ireland, to Milesius of Spain. Likewise, Good John's mother, Agnes O'Cahan, springs from the line of Milesius, more along Irish lines. In another development, John's sixth-great-grandson Somhairle Buighe MacDonnell married Mary O'Neill, whose roots can be traced back through Naill of the Nine Hostages to the dawn of the Irish nation.

In this volume, I start with the Hebrews and proceed through the Trojans, the Scandinavians and the Irish, finally arriving at the Scots, some of whom eventually emigrated to North America, whence I come.

My great-grandfather, Leonard J. Passmore, wrote in his diary that his father-in-law John Walter Banta met "a lovely Scotch girl" named Rebecca Angelina McDonald in Texas, and married her. Interestingly, the definition of "Scotch" is not as clear-cut as we would like to believe. Of her forefathers (as far back as King Ivar II), five were born in the American colonies, twelve in Ireland, and only ten in "Scotland" (that is, the Western Isles). From around the 5th century AD until the 11th century, the Irish began to occupy lands and islands around western Scotland. Beginning in the 8th or 9th century, the Vikings began to intermarry with the Irish. Scotland itself underwent a transformation from its Pictish origins to the Gaelic culture of the Irish who more or less conquered it.

A note about the numbering system: all numbers refer to the number of generations from Adam. We begin this volume with the descendants of Noah, progressing from Shem through Zarah (#11-#24), on to the Trojans (#25-#32) and the Scandinavians (#33-#81), up until the Vikings in Ireland (#82-#92). From there we skip back to the descendants of Japheth (Shem's older brother), among whom was Milesius (number 36 without a hashtag), who migrated to Ireland. Beginning with King Conn of the Hundred Battles (82-m), the -m suffix refers to "descendants of Milesius." The Irish began intermarrying with the Scots, so we will continue through the kings of Argyle, the kings of Scotland (to 121-m), then back again to the descendants of Vikings (#93 onwards, with hashtags). Notice the Viking line continues into the North American branch of the McDonalds, who were really hybrids, the Isles being technically part of Scotland, but also close to Ireland.

Sorry for all the strange, unpronounceable names.

Part 1
The Hebrews

Let's start at the beginning (what a very good place to start)! Of course, the story of the human race begins with Adam and Eve (that is, unless you believe we evolved from monkeys, which I would be embarrassed to admit, if I were you). Most of our first fathers were recorded in the Old Testament, though the names of their wives were not always so well documented. Even in the case of our First Mother, rumor has it that she was preceded by a woman named Lilith, Adam's first wife. Whatever. The important thing, for Adam's descendants, is that he married Eve.

For the first eighteen hundred years or so, everything went along without a hitch (except for that nasty incident between Cain and Abel). As you can see from the ancestry chart on the following page, there were ten generations from Adam until Noah. That's when calamity struck. The Great Flood. Every civilization on Earth has a similar account, that is, an inundation that destroyed (many or) all the people on Earth, survived by one man and his family.

That brings us to Mount Ararat, somewhere in Turkey. After disembarking, Noah doled out portions of the Earth to each of his three sons: Shem, Ham and Japheth. The children of Shem gave rise to the Persians, Assyrians, Babylonians, Lydians, and Syrians. The children of Ham gave rise to the Ethiopians, Egyptians, Libyans and Canaanites. The children of Japheth gave rise to the Cimmerians (who migrated to Western Europe as we know it), Scythians, Medes, Greeks, Turks, Slavs and Etruscans. In this volume, we will take special interest in the children of Shem and Japheth.

As for the children of Shem, they gave rise to the "Semites." Through Shem's great-grandson Eber, we now know them as the Hebrews. Ten generations after Noah, we come to Abraham, and from his great-grandson Judah comes Zarah, whose descendants became the Trojans.

We wouldn't want Ham to feel left out, now would we? Not to worry. His line contributes in a major way to the Kings of Troy, not only through Hercules, but also through Atlas. And why should mourning become Electra? Rather she should rejoice, being the mother of many nations.

As for Japheth, his son Magog gave rise to the Scythians, who lived in the region of modern-day Ukraine. Some of these people migrated to Spain, and eventually to Ireland. It is from these Irish immigrants that Scotland became a nation. (Ironically, during the English colonization of Ulster in the 17th century, many Scots re-migrated to what is now Northern Ireland.) In addition, we shall see later in our narrative that Odin, himself a descendant of Shem, migrated through Russia and Northern Europe to Scandinavia.

Well, let's get started.

Table 1. Descendants of Adam and Eve.

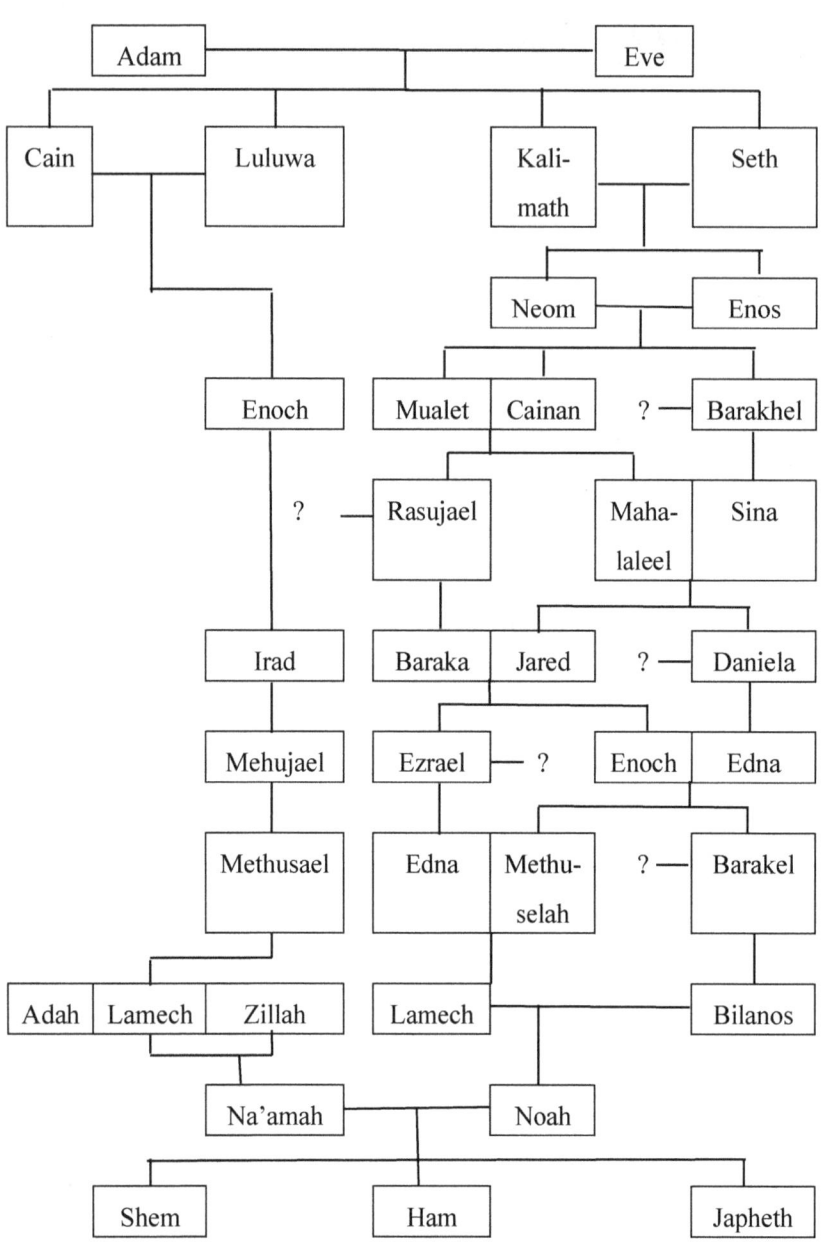

Genesis 4:1-22   Genesis 4:25-32

from Shem to Darda

#20 Abraham

As we have seen, Abraham was born in the tenth generation from Noah, or the twentieth generation from Adam. The story of Abraham and his wife Sarah illustrates a number of important points.

First, but probably not foremost, is the development of family values and marriage laws in the early Chaldean region. It is common, even today, for Arab men to desire to have a male heir. With the advent of Islam, a man whose wife does not produce such a male heir may (with his first wife's permission) try again with a second wife. If that fails, he may take a third wife, and so on up until the fourth wife. (King Henry VIII of England tried a variation on this theme, much to the regret of his many wives.) But this was before Islam, and Abraham's wife Sarah was not able to bear him a son; at least not at first.

Thus Abraham adopted his manservant Eliezer. An adopted son, after all, is better than having no heir. Then came a blessing, of sorts. Sarah's maidservant Hagar bore Abraham a natural son called Ishmael. This was a good thing, but when Sarah's own son Isaac was finally born, it resulted in squabbling over who was the rightful heir. Was it Ishmael, the older son? Or was it Isaac, the son of Abraham's lawful wife? Sadly, the discussion continues to this very day.

The second important point that the story of Abraham illustrates is that of his faith in God. Born in Ur of the Chaldees, Abraham left that region and migrated westward with his flocks. A man of great faith, Abraham trusted (somewhat) God's promise that he would give him a son. God made a covenant with Abraham and instructed him to seal the covenant in blood: all the men of his household, and all the men from that day forward, were to perform the Eighth Day ritual. Ach! Then, even at a ripe old age, when it was beyond the manner of women with Sarah, God finally delivered on His promise. Then the real test began.

God told Abraham to sacrifice his son Isaac, which Abraham set out to do. That must have been something to behold, after waiting one hundred years for his son to be born, then having to build an altar and slay him with a knife, but Abraham did as he was told. At the last moment, a ram came out of the bush, and Isaac was spared. Abraham believed God, and it was reckoned unto him as righteousness.

#21 Isaac

We can learn five lessons from the life of Isaac, Abraham's son. The first lesson was perhaps inadvertently learned by Isaac when he was very young. Can you imagine how he felt when he learned that *he* was to be made a sacrificial lamb, when his father Abraham took him to that place on the mountain? In the same way we are to present our bodies as a living sacrifice, holy, acceptable to God, which is our reasonable service.

Second, Abraham commanded his servant never to take a wife for Isaac from among the Canaanites, because of their sinfulness. (Surely the behavior of his nephew Lot's daughters, who in their wickedness seduced their own father, was fresh in his memory.) With this in mind the servant went to Abraham's brother, who was still living in Chaldea. God guided the servant to Rebekah (the namesake of our own Rebecca McDonald!), who offered water not only to the servant, but also to his ten camels. Thus Isaac married his own second cousin, the granddaughter of Abraham's brother.

The third lesson is that we should not play favorites. Rebekah suffered from infertility, similar to the problem of her mother-in-law Sarah, yet Isaac fervently pleaded with God to give him a son. God was most generous and granted him twins: Esau and Jacob. The problem was that Isaac loved Esau, a hairy hunter, because he brought home venison to eat. Rebekah loved Jacob, a smooth-skinned, mild-mannered boy. The rivalry between the two brothers led Rebekah ultimately to deceive Isaac, who in his old age had become blind. She dressed Jacob up in furs and tricked Isaac into giving his final blessing to Jacob rather than to Esau.

The fourth lesson is that we should submit to the will of God. While the two brothers were still in Rebekah's womb, God sent her a prophecy that the older would wind up serving the younger. This is not to say that God was playing favorites; just that He knew what would happen. As it turned out, Esau came back one day from hunting and found Jacob making porridge in the kitchen. Jacob said he would give him some porridge, if Esau would sell him his birthright. Technically, it was not necessary for Rebekah to trick Isaac into blessing Jacob instead of Esau. He had already given up his rightful position as the elder brother. Lo and behold, the prophecy had come to pass!

The final lesson has to do with the wells of water that Isaac dug. Sojourning in the plains of Gerar, Isaac found that many of the wells that his father Abraham dug had been filled in with earth by the Philistines. Isaac re-opened the wells, but his herdsmen got into trouble with the locals, who argued that the water was theirs. Instead of fighting, Isaac merely moved to another location. This happened again and again, until finally the people of Gerar stopped bothering him. Blessed are the peacemakers, for they shall be called the sons of God.

#22 Jacob

Jacob's issues with his brother Esau led him to travel abroad, to his uncle Laban's house. On the way, he stopped at a rest stop. There he lay his head on a stone and fell into a dream. (Some say he had placed twelve stones around him for protection.) He dreamt of a ladder with angels going up and down into Heaven. In his dream, God promised Jacob that he would protect him and his offspring, and the land on which he lay. When he awoke, the twelve stones had fused into one, which he set up as an altar. He called this place Bethel, and the field would eventually become the location of the Temple Mount in Jerusalem. (This stone will show up later in Scotland… don't forget!)

When Jacob arrived at his uncle's house he met Rachel and fell in love with her. He told Laban that he would work for seven years, if he would let him marry Rachel. Laban agreed, but when the seven years passed, it was Rachel's older sister Leah who was given to him to marry. Jacob did not complain; during that time four sons were born (including Judah), but he didn't give up. He offered to work seven more years to win Rachel's hand in marriage.

Having finished his second term of indentured servitude, Jacob set out with his wives and concubines (his wives' handmaidens) to return home. On the way, he learned that his brother Esau was waiting with four hundred men to attack him. That night, Jacob wrestled with his angel. "Jacob was left alone; a man wrestled with him, until the rising of the dawn." If he was alone, then who was the "man"? Was he an angel? Or was he Jacob's alter ego? Was Jacob still Jacob? Or had he become Israel? Jacob the Hero meets Jacob the Trickster. Every man wrestles with his angel at one point in his life. Jacob won the wrestling match, but he suffered a dislocated hip in the fight. The next day he bowed down to Esau, melting his brother's heart.

Rachel grew old and died, but Jacob loved her son Joseph, for whom he made a many-colored coat. Joseph dreamt that the sun, moon, stars, and wheat sheaves all bowed down to him. His brothers grew jealous and sold him into slavery, dousing the coat in goat's blood to trick their father into believing he had died. Jacob mourned for twenty-two years, during which Joseph wound up in Egypt, in the Pharaoh's dungeons. There, he interpreted Pharaoh's dreams of famine and plenty, so Pharaoh made him viceroy of Egypt.

When famine came in the land, Jacob sent his ten sons to Egypt to buy food. Joseph recognized them, but they didn't know he was their brother. He invited all his family to join him in Egypt, which they did. Pharaoh asked Jacob how old he was (he was 130). Then Jacob blessed Pharaoh, and the famine ended.

#23 Judah

It was Judah's idea to sell his brother Joseph into slavery. Actually, the idea was more appealing than to kill him, as he was, after all, their brother. More than that, having seen how his father treated his mother Leah, Judah undertook to marry a Canaanite woman, the daughter of Shua, an act that was not permitted the offspring of Abraham. This marriage produced three sons – Er, Onan and Shelah.

Now Judah arranged for a woman named Tamar to marry his oldest son, but Er was so evil that God took his life. Judah then commanded Onan to marry Tamar (as was the custom), but he refused because any heir would be that of his brother, so God killed him, too. Judah asked Tamar to wait until Shelah was old enough to marry, but by that time Judah's wife had died. Seeing her father-in-law go out to shear his sheep, Tamar approached him dressed as a harlot, and took a few items from him for collateral. Thus she became pregnant with the twins Perez and Zarah. When the twins were born, Judah softened up toward Tamar.

While under the protection of Pharaoh, Joseph demanded that his ten brothers bring their youngest brother Benjamin to Egypt. The oldest brother, Reuben, offered up his own sons as hostages. 'Kill my two sons if I do not bring him back to you. Put him in my hands, and I will bring him back to you.' Jacob rejected this offer, as Reuben could not take responsibility by himself. In order to save his family from starvation, Judah stepped in and took personal responsibility. 'Send the boy with me, and we will arise and go ... I will be a pledge of his safety. From my hand you shall require him. If I do not bring him back to you and set him before you, then let me bear the blame forever.'

Thus Judah assumed preeminence over his brothers and became the spokesman for the family in Egypt. Afterwards Jacob blessed him, saying, "The scepter shall not depart from Judah, nor the ruler's staff from between his feet."

Judah's life gives us an example of how God can transform a person for His purpose. Judah was the fourth son of an unloved wife. He sinned by going in to a person he believed to be a harlot (but who was in fact his own son's widow). Not only did God convict him of his unrighteousness, but He also led Judah to repentance. Judah's descendants included King David as well as Christ Himself.

#24 Zarah

In the book of Genesis (38), we read about the birth of Judah and Tamar's twin sons.

> And it came to pass in the time of her travail, that, behold, twins were in her womb. And it came to pass, when she travailed, that *the one* put out *his* hand: and the midwife took and bound upon his hand a scarlet thread, saying, This came out first. And it came to pass, as he drew back his hand, that, behold, his brother came out: and she said, How hast thou broken forth? *this* breach *be* upon thee: therefore his name was called Pharez. And afterward came out his brother, that had the scarlet thread upon his hand: and his name was called Zarah. (KJV)

Judah's surviving youngest son Shelah, whose mother was Bath-Shua might have claimed to inherit the Royal bloodline of the nation of Israel, as per the prophecy, but his mother was a Canaanite (whom he met in a town called Adulla through his friend Hirah). The problem was resolved by the birth of these twins, but a new problem arose: which was the eldest? Eventually Pharez was declared the rightful heir, and from him descended the official branch of the Tribe of Judah.

How do you think Zarah would react to this decision? It stands to reason that his descendants did not accept this ruling and found a way to escape their bondage in Egypt, before the Exodus of the main body of Hebrews. As the genealogy of Zarah apparently ceases with the third generation, his descendants must have left Egypt during the time of Israel's captivity. How did they escape? Where did they go?

Pre-Exodus Migrations

We are told in 1 Chronicles 2 that Zarah had five sons: Zimri, Ethan, Heman, Calcol and Dara. History and tradition record that most of them decided to flee to some new lands where they could be free of Egyptian rule. Of these five, we know of at least two groups which escaped Egypt and fled in different directions across the Mediterranean Sea. Calcol and his followers fled to Greece and founded the city of Athens. Dara (Darda) and his followers went north and became the ancestors of the Trojans. We do not know what happened to the others.

However, Homer records the ancestral lineage of Troy as Cronus – Zeus – Dardanus – Erichthonius – Tros – Ilus – Laomedon – Priam. What then can we make of Darda's supposed descent from Zeus and Cronus?

#25 Darda

The city of Troy was destroyed in the famous Trojan War, so we know little of their mythology, aside from artifacts which have been dug up. What we know of Greek mythology comes largely from the account of the war written by Homer. Yet when we think about it, many ancient "gods" were in fact humans who had been deified by their admiring descendants.

I.P. Cory, in *Ancient Fragments*, recounted that the Sibylline Oracles (written by Amonian priestesses) "named Kronus, Titan, and Iapetus (Japheth) as the three sons of the Patriarch (Noah), who governed the world in the tenth generation after the Flood, and mentioned the division of the world into three parts," that is, unto Shem, Ham and Japheth. (Cory, p. 76)

The Phoenician historian Sanchoniathon (fl. 1200 B.C.) wrote, "And when a plague and mortality happened, Kronus offered up his only son as a sacrifice to his father Ouranos, and circumcised himself, and compelled his allies to do the same (Cory, pp. 16-17)... For Kronus (or Saturn), whom the Phoenicians call Israel, and who after his death was deified, and instated in the planet which bears his name, when he was king, had by a nymph of the country, called Anobret (possibly Sarah), an only son, who, on that account is styled Ieoud" (*Yakhid*, meaning only-begotten). (Isaac Preston Cory, *Ancient Fragments*, London: Reeves, 1828, pp. 21-22).

This Phoenician account strongly resembles the story of Abraham, but if Kronus referred to Israel, it would likely mean a member of the *nation* of Israel, rather than the *person* of Israel (i.e., Jacob). It would also be possible that Oceanus, who married Tethys, could refer to Noah himself, as Tethri was one of the names of his wife (see Utley, "The One Hundred Three Names of Noah's Wife"), though Noah is generally assumed to be Uranus.

Speaking of wives, Kronus married Rhea, whose name could be a portmanteau derived from Jacob's wives Rachel and Leah. Ze-us, the offspring of Kronus and Rhea, was probably a Hellenized form of Ze-rah, the offspring of Judah (of the tribe of Israel) and Tamar. It is my contention that the children of Zarah who escaped Egypt did so without taking much of their written history with them. The succeeding generations of Greeks (and also Trojans) had to rely on oral tradition, and from this sketchy memory invented their own unique mythology. (It is interesting to note that even the Egyptians, in their records of the first demigods, list Hephaestus, Helios, Kronus, Ares, Heracles, Apollo and Zeus among their earliest kings, before the Deluge. These, however, began with a long period of thirty dynasties which covered 36,525 years.) (Cory, p. 111)

Well, Troy wasn't built in a day. We do know it was built on the Dardanelles, most likely by Zarah's son Dardanus, a Hebrew who came out of Egypt. We will read more about Troy after a brief interlude.

from Ham to Priam

The children of Ham had quite a lot to do with events which followed. Let's see how this branch of Noah's family developed, *mythologically*, into the ancestors of Troy. If you say, "Wait a minute – the names of the *Greek* characters don't always match up with Biblical names," you are right. But the names in Greek myths don't always matter: it is the *characters*, and what they do, that counts.

Ham and Rhea   One of the many names of Noah's wife was Titea, and from her the Titans got their name. Ham's wife Noela was with him in the ark. Genesis records their children (sons) as Cush, Mizraim, Phut and Canaan. Nimrod, a son of Cush, "began to be a mighty one in the earth." Un-fortunately, he was so mighty that he built the Tower that confused our languages.

Japheth's eldest son Gomer was the first king of Italy. After Gomer died, Ham went there and usurped the throne. Noah, thinking Gomer was still alive, went for a visit and found that the kingdom had fallen into disarray. He banished Ham to Sicily and set things in order, ruling jointly with a brother of Nimrod named Saturn. No one knows what happened to Noela.

Ham's younger sister Rhea had been married to a King Hammon, whom she left because he was having an affair with another woman called Almanthea. Rhea went to Sicily and married Ham.

Isis and Osiris   Ham and Rhea had a son called Osiris and a daughter called Isis, who got married. Together they ruled Egypt. Their eldest son was Hercules, who appears as "Lehabim" in Genesis 10:13. This means Osiris must have been the same person as Mizraim, the son of Ham and Noela.

Hercules and Araxa   One day Osiris went to Scythia and found that his son Hercules had fallen in love with Araxa, who was likely a descendant of Araxa the Great, a daughter of Noah. Hercules and Araxa had a son called Tuscus who "much later" became king of Italy, and the province of Tuscany was named after him. Hercules, meanwhile lived peaceably in France for a while, then he went to Italy, which he ruled for 20 years.

Hercules and Omphale   Hercules also had relations with a woman named Omphale. They had a son known as Athus the Great of Phrygia (in west-central Turkey). His fourth-great grandson Athus welcomed Dardanus, who married his daughter Batea, in Phrygia.

Priam   That brings us (after five generations) to Priam, who was king of Troy when the Greeks laid siege to that beautiful city.

Table 2. Descendants of Noah and his Wife, featuring Ham.
(Dotted lines indicate more than one generation.)

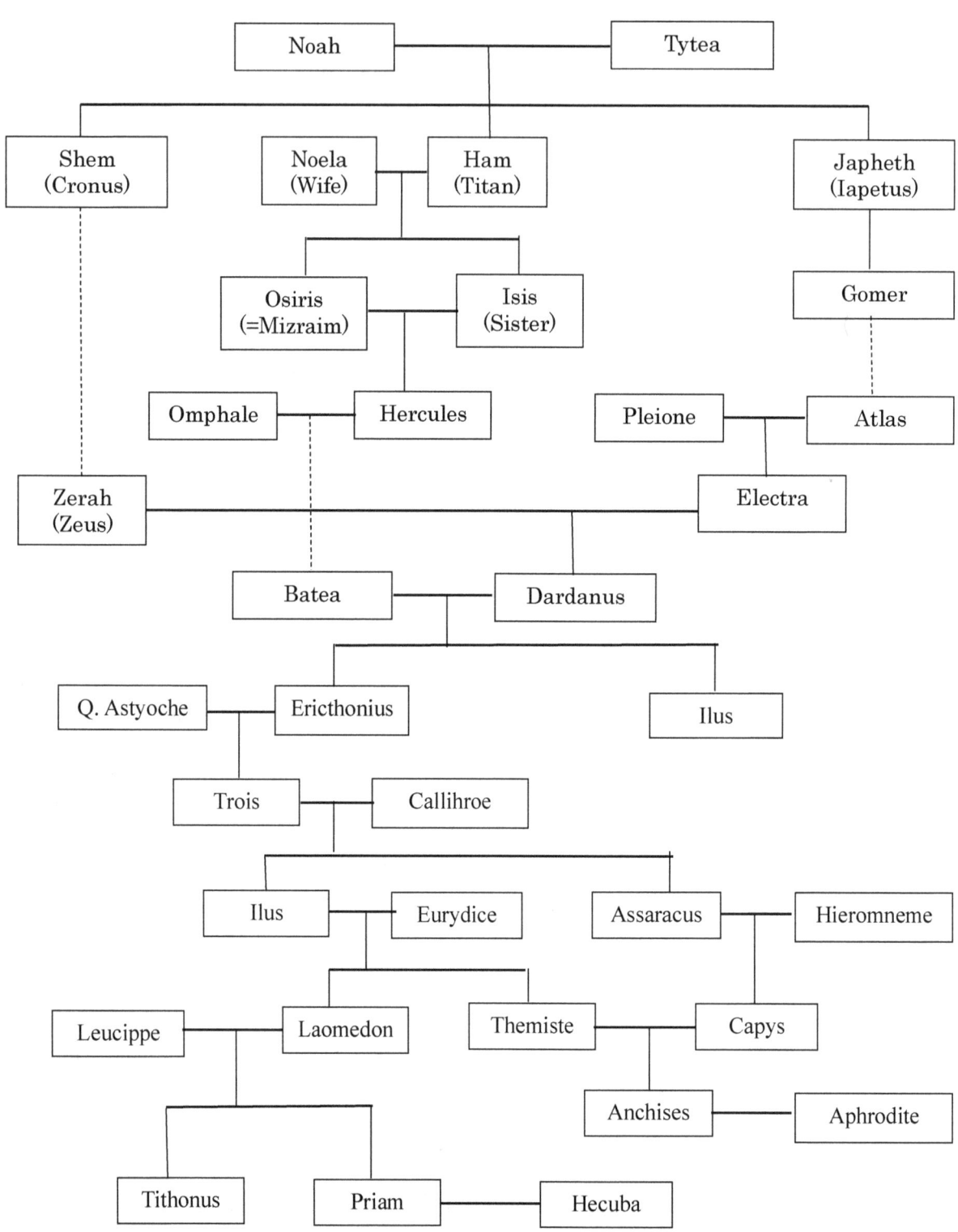

from Japheth to Miles

Established wisdom holds that Miles(ius) descended from Noah's eldest son Japheth, through his son Magog, whose son was Baoth. Different sources for Magog's descendants do not all agree.*

The Bible tells us that Shem had 5 sons; Ham had 4 sons; Japheth had 7 sons. However Augustine, in *The City of God* (*De Civitate Dei*) XVI, claims that Shem had 27 sons; Ham had 31; Japheth had 15. The apparent contradiction is straightened out in Genesis 10, which names the *descendants*, rather than the *sons*, of Shem, Ham and Japheth:

Shem (Total = 27)	Ham (Total = 31)	Japheth (Total = 15)
Elam	Cush	Gomer
Asshur	Seba, Havilah,	Ashkenaz, Riphath,
Arphaxad	Sabtah, Sabtechah,	Tigermah
Salah	Raamah	Magog
Eber	Shebah, Dedan	Madal
Peleg,	Nimrod	Javan
Joktan	Mizraim	Elishah, Tarshish,
Almodad, Sheleth,	Ludim, Anamim,	Katim, Dodanim
Hazarmaveth, Jerah,	Lehabim, Naphtuhim	Tubal
Hadoram, Uzal,	Pathrusim, Cashuhim,	Meshech
Diklah, Obal,	Caphtorim	Tiras
Abimael, Sheba,	Phut	
Ophir, Havilah,	Canaan	
Johab	Sidon, Heth, (Jebusites,	
Lud	Amorites, Girgasites,	
Aram	Hivites, Arkites,	
Uz, Hul, Gether, Mash	Sinites, Arvadites,	
	Zemarites, Hamathites)	

* The Irish *Book of Invasions* (*Lebor Gabala Erenn*) lists his sons as Baath, Jobhath and Fathochta. Johannes Magnus (1488-1544), Archbishop of Uppsala, thought that Magog migrated to Scandinavia by way of Finland 88 years after the flood, and that his sons were named Suenno (namesake of Sweden), Gog, Ubbo (namesake of Uppsala), Thor, and German. Here we see that Shem and his descendants numbered 27; Ham and his descendants, 31; Japheth and his descendants, 15. The grand total of all those descendants of Noah comes out to 73.

Genesis (10:32) goes on to state that "These are the families of the sons of Noah, after their generations, in their nations: and by these were the nations divided in the earth after the flood." Other references in Genesis refer to their languages: "By these [sons of Japheth] were the isles of the Gentiles divided in their lands, every one after his tongue" (10:5); "These are the sons of Ham, after their families, after their tongues" (10:20); "These are the sons of Shem, after their families, after their tongues" (10:31). In Chapter 11, we read the story of the Tower of Babel.

The total of 73 "tongues" (of Noah's descendants) would account for the 72 languages which resulted from the "confusion" brought about at the building of Nimrod's Tower, plus one, the original Adamic language. Some say that Eber, Shem's great-grandson, did not participate in the building of the Tower, so his language (Hebrew*) was spared. However, this point is also challenged in the *Scholars' Primer* (*Auraicept na Neces*), a 7th century description of the Irish language. The *Primer* claims that Eber was among six leaders who built the Tower of Nimrod.** John O'Hart, in *Irish Pedigrees* (p. 30) claims that it was Magog's son Baoth (or Baath), King of Scythia, who took no part in the Tower, hence the Celtic language was preserved.

After the Whirlwind, King Baoth's son Fenius Farsaid went down to Shinan to study the different languages. The *Primer* says he was one of three sages that led the seventy-two poets in their study. Fenius Farsaidh (whose last name means "Pharisee") was reputed to have discovered alphabets, that is, Hebrew, Greek, and Latin, and to have invented the Irish *Beith Luis Nin*, or Ogham vowels, as found in the Books of Woods (for they are metaphorically named after trees). (Fenius' brother Cadmus was the first to take an alphabetic writing system to the Greeks.) Afterwards, Fenius' grandson Gaedel set out to determine the best features of all the languages and combine them into one, a kind of ancient Esperanto, which became the Gaelic (named for Gaedel) language. The most elegant form of this language, *Bearla na Fileadh*, was the secret language of the Poets. A lower form of the language, *Gnaith-Bearla*, was intended for commoners to use, and evolved into modern Irish.

* The original language would have changed over time. The Deluge took place in 2348 BC, some 1656 years after Adam. Take a moment to think about how much English, or any language for that matter, has changed since 366 A.D., some 1656 years ago. For example, Latin has changed into Italian, Spanish, French, Portuguese and Romanian.

** "Six principal chiefs by whom the Tower was made, to vit, Eber Mac Saile, Grecus Mac Corner whence are the Greeks, and Latinus son of Faunus whence are the Latins, Riabad Scot son of Gomer, Nimrod son of Cush, and Fenius Farsaidh… there are 943 years from the dispersion of the Tower till Aeneas married Lavinia."

Two Scotas

At this point we need to mention two women named Scota. Although they lived centuries apart, each was important to our narrative. Each was the daughter of a different Egyptian pharaoh. Each married a different descendant of Japheth. One lent her name to Scythia; the other to Scotland.

Some say our first Scota was married to Fenius Farsaidh, but it is far more likely that she married his son Niul. Fenius had banished Niul from Crete for killing his brother. He made his way to Egypt where he befriended Pharaoh Semenkhkare, son of Akhenaton. Since Niul was now fluent in 72 languages, he would prove very useful as an interpreter and advisor to Cinqueris (another name for this pharaoh, 11th Dynasty). He was not only granted a position as minister (which included a villa on the Red Sea), but also the hand of the Princess Scota in marriage.

Now it just so happened that this Scota was the same person who had found baby Moses adrift in a basket and took him into pharaoh's household. When Niul and Scota's son Goedel (Gaythelos) was bitten by a snake, it stood to reason that Moses should seek to heal him.

Scota and Gaythelos

Our second person of interest was Scota Tephi, "daughter" of Nectaebus and sister of King Solomon's queen. This Scota married Milesius (#36), and together they had eight sons, including Amergin (the druid), Ir (namesake of Ireland) and Heremon. They came to Ireland in 1699 B.C.

Heremon eventually became king of all Ireland and married Scota's sister Tea Tephi. Some, however, suggest that both Scota and Tea could have been daughters of King Zedekiah, whisked to safety out of the hands of Nebuchadnezzar to become wards of the house of Pharaoh (Jer. 43:5-7). This makes some sense, in that Tea is said to have been the daughter of *Lughaidh*, which in Irish means "God's House." Not only that, but it doesn't seem logical that an Egyptian princess would have been in possession of the Stone of Destiny, which was first brought to Ireland by Scota.

The Stone of Destiny

Part 2
Troy

As I mentioned before, the mythology of Troy is pretty much lost to us. All that remains of Troy is what was recorded afterwards by the Greeks. After all, the people who win wars get to write the history of those wars, and if Troy was wiped out by Greece, then "to the victors went the spoils."

Luckily, the Greeks were pretty good myth-makers. One myth refers to Aeneas, a son of Aphrodite. He married first Cruesa, but she disappeared during their escape from the burning city of Troy. Later he married Lavinia. Children of his second marriage to Lavinia were ancestors of the Kings of Alba Longa in Italy. These eventually included Romulus and Remus, the legendary founders of the city of Rome. The children of his first marriage to Creusa were ancestors of the Kings of Britain.

Brutus was a great-grandson of Aeneas, who had settled in Italy on the banks of the Tiber River. When he was a teenager, Brutus went hunting with his father Silvius, whom he accidentally killed with an arrow. As punishment, he was exiled from Italy and went back to Greece. There he met a group of Trojans who had been enslaved after the war. He became their leader; they revolted against their masters and fled Greece. At length Brutus and his followers came to a deserted island. On this island he found a temple dedicated to the goddess Diana. There he performed sacred rituals and fell asleep in front of a statue of the goddess. In his dream, Diana showed him visions of an island called Albion in the western ocean, home to but a few giants. He understood by this dream that he was to lead his followers there and establish a new nation. Eventually they came to Albion, where they were confronted by the giants, descendants of Gog and Magog. They defeated the giants, and Brutus founded a city on the banks of the River Thames. He named this city New Troy, which was later corrupted to Trinovantum; today it is called London.

A third myth arises from Creusa's uncle Tithonus, who married Eos, the goddess of the dawn. Their son Memnon fought on the side of Troy during the war, but he was killed by Achilles. Memnon married Sibil; their son Thor was the ancestor (twenty-three generations removed) of Odin, the Norse god whom today we remember every Wednesday.

Aeneas Carries Anchises out of Troy

Table 3. The Mythological Kings.

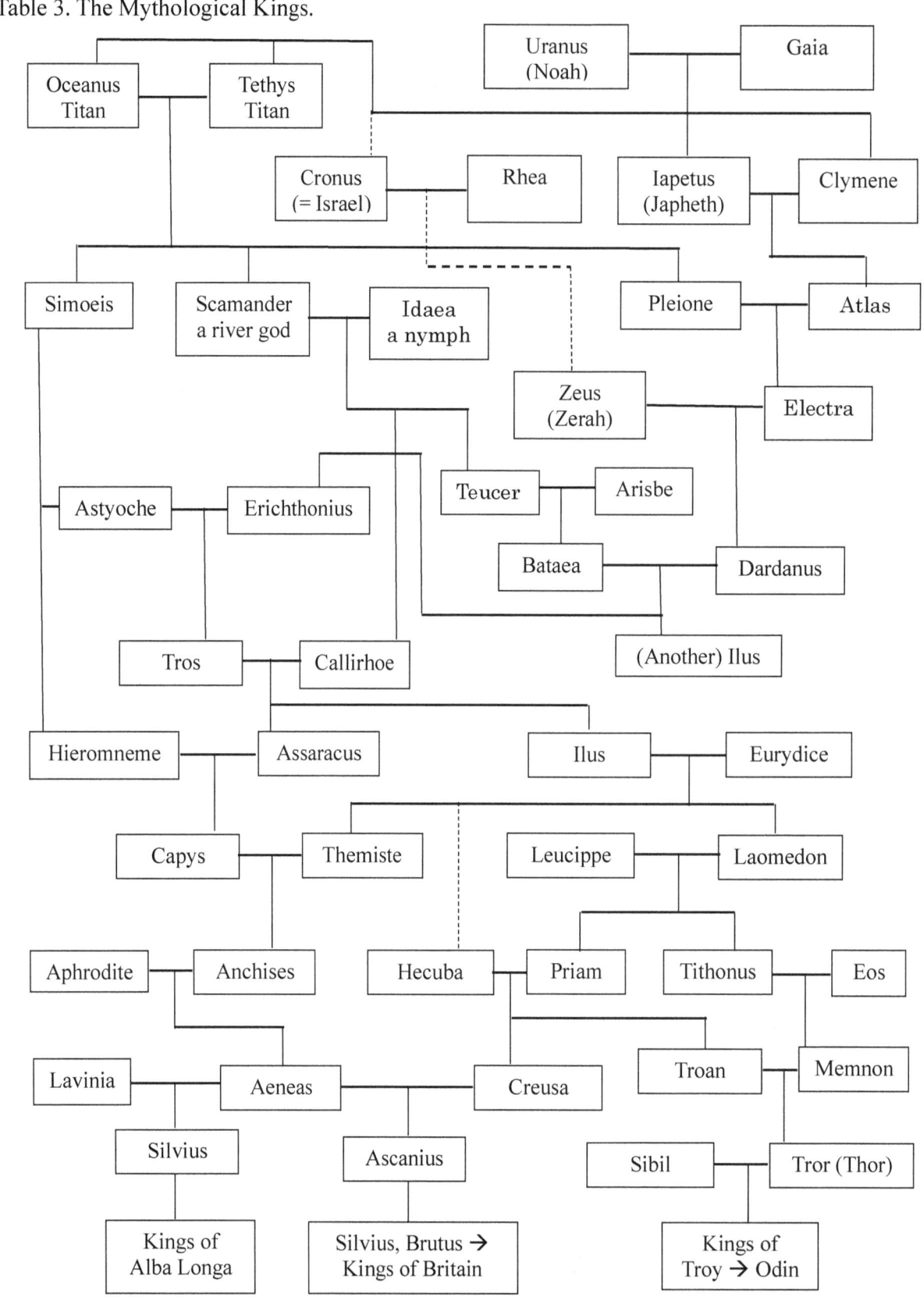

from Darda to Thor

#25 Dardanus

The Dardanelles is a narrow strait of water in Turkey that links the Black Sea with the Aegean Sea. It is also known as the Strait of Gallipoli. In ancient times, it was known as the Hellespont, after a girl named Helle who was drowned there after falling off a magical ram that had golden fleece. Today, the strait is named for Dardanus, son of Zarah (#25) and Electra.

When the sons of Zarah (Zimri, Ethan, Heman, Calcol and Dara) escaped from Egypt, Calcol's group went to Mycenae, in southern Greece; then they founded the city of Athens.* Those who traveled with Darda went northwest, into Turkey. There Darda was welcomed by King Teucer. This king was very generous, not only giving him land but also the hand of his daughter Batea in marriage. They had two sons, Ilus and Erichthonius. When King Teucer died, Dardanus took over as king.

King Teucer was originally from the island of Crete, but he left when a famine came in the land. When he and his followers first came to Troas (in southwestern Turkey) they were bothered by a plague of mice. Teucer had been advised by an oracle to build his settlement in a place "where the earth-born should attack them during the night." Thus he established his capital, called Hamaxitus, and he built a temple to Apollo Sminthius, the "destroyer of mice." Since Teucer didn't have a natural son (Batea was his only child), the kingdom fell to Dardanus when Teucer died. The Trojans often referred to themselves as Teucrians, acknowledging that King Teucer was their first king.

The Fall of Troy

* The city of Athens derives its name from the goddess of wisdom, Athena, who became the city's patron goddess after a contest with Poseidon. The two gods competed for the honor of becoming the patron god of the city, each offering gifts to the Athenians. Poseidon hit the ground with his trident and created a spring, showing that he would offer significant naval power. Athena offered an olive tree, a symbol of prosperity and peace. The Athenians, led by King Cecrops I (or Calcol), decided to accept Athena's gift, making her the patron goddess.

#26 Erichthonius

Dardanus and Batea had two sons, Ilus and Erichthonius, but Ilus died, leaving Erichthonius to inherit the kingdom. Erichthonius married the Naiad Astyoche, daughter of the river-god Simoeis. They had a son named Tros, who would later give his name to the Trojan people.

When the gods took sides in the Trojan War, the brothers Simoeis and Scamander (also named after a river) supported the Trojans. Scamander called for his brother's help in fighting Achilles: "Fill your streams with water from your springs… stand high in a great wave… so we can stop this savage man who in his strength is raging like the gods." Before Simoeis could respond, Hephaestus saved Achilles by spewing flame on the river Scamander.

King Erichthonius became the wealthiest of all kings. He had perhaps as many as 3000 mares, which would feed with their foals upon the lush meadows of his kingdom.

The god Boreas observed the mares, and taking the form of a stallion, he did mate with a number of them. These mares gave birth to 12 fillies, horses with unmatched speed, which could course over the top of a field of wheat without damaging a single ear, or could gallop over the sea without getting their feet wet.

Horses were closely associated with the House of Troy, and later when Erichthonius' grandson Ganymede (son of Tros) was abducted by Zeus, the god sent Hermes to take Tros some swift horses as a form of compensation. Hermes also assured Tros that Ganymede would be immortal and would become the cupbearer of the gods, a position of great distinction.

Is it any wonder the Trojans were deceived by the now-famous Trojan Horse?

Zeus and Ganymede

#27 Tros Acadia

Tros was born in Dardania in about 1375 BC. He was a son of Erichthonius and Astyoche. When Erichthonius died, Tros inherited the throne of Troy, to which he gave his name.

Tros married Callirhoe, daughter of the river-god Scamander and the Nymph Idaea. Callirhoe was born in Minor, Russia, in 1345 BC. This alternate ancestry chart of Callirhoe Ilium shows her descent from Judah, son of Jacob:

Table 4: Callirhoe's Ancestors

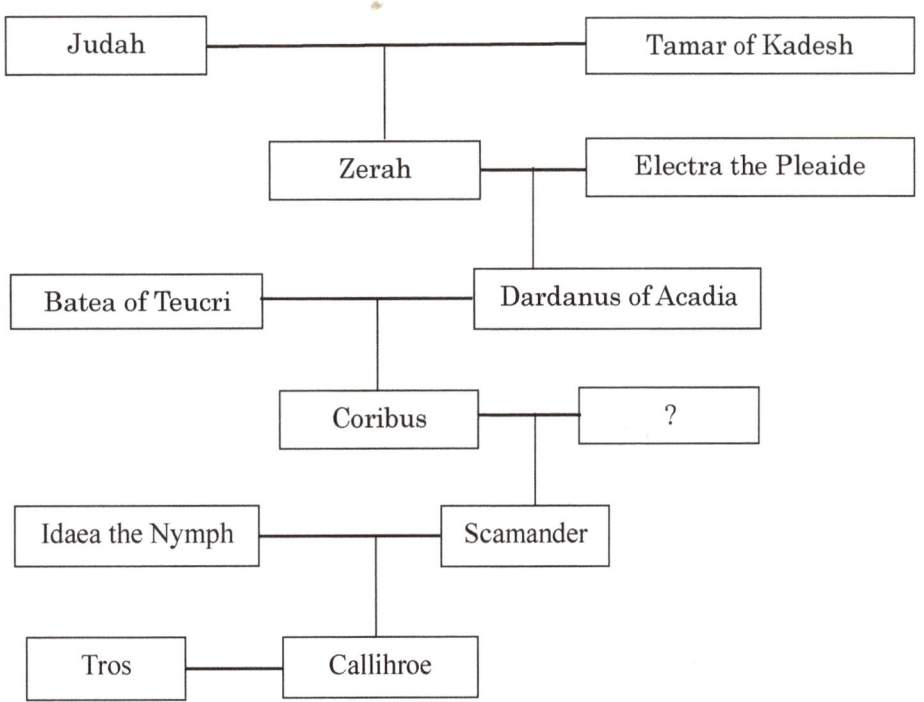

Tros and Callihroe had three sons: Ilus, Assaracus, and Ganymede. When Zeus abducted Ganymede, Tros grieved for his son, but Hermes took him a gift of horses to console him.

Callirhoe

#28 Ilus Troy

Ilus was the eldest son of Tros of Dardania and brother of Assaracus and Ganymede. Every four years the King of Phrygia held games. Ilus got first place in wrestling and received a prize of fifty youths and maidens as his reward. The king, on the advice of an oracle, also gave him a dappled cow and asked him to establish a city wherever that cow should lie down. Ilus then prayed to Zeus for a sign and at once saw the Palladium, a three-cubit high wooden statue, fallen from heaven and lying before his tent. He was immediately blinded, for humans were not allowed to look on the image. Later he regained his sight after making offerings to the goddess Athena.

This is how Ilus became the founder of the city called Ilios, which he named after himself. When this became the chief city of the Trojan people it was also often called Troy, the name by which it is best known today. Ilus preferred his new city of Ilium to Dardania and on his father's death he remained there, passing the rule of Dardania on to his younger brother Assaracus, thus the Trojans were split into two kingdoms.

Ilus married Eurydice, daughter of Adrastus, a prince of Argos, and Amphithea of Argos. Their son Laomedon would inherit the kingdom from his father. Their daughter Themiste married Ilus' nephew Capys (of the Dardanian line). Ilus' daughter Telecleia married Cisseus of Thrace, who had given Capys and Themiste's son Anchises a bowl engraved with figures, as a token of their friendship.

Ilus died in 1279 BC, succeeded by his son Laomedon.

Eurydice of Troy

#29 Laomedon of Troy

Laomedon was the son and successor of King Ilus. He married Strymo, Placia or Leucippe, or possibly all of them at different times. With Leucippe, he was the father of Priam (see #31 below) and many other sons. He had at least one daughter, named Hesione. Another son named Tithonus (see #32 below) was abducted by Eos, goddess of the dawn, and taken to Ethiopia, where the goddess bore him a son called Memnon.

Laomedon was known as the king, for his arrogance and impiety and who refused to honor his promises. Poseidon and Apollo had rebelled against Zeus, and as their punishment they had to work for a mortal for one year. The two gods disguised themselves as construction workers, and were hired to work alongside Aeacus to build the walls of Troy. Poseidon and Apollo requested the vine of gold as payment for their work. Laomedon agreed, but after the gods finished building the wall, Laomedon refused to pay their wages. In revenge, Apollo caused a plague within the city, while Poseidon sent a sea-monster to ravage the Trojan countryside.

The oracles told Laomedon that the land would be spared if the king sacrificed his daughter to the sea-monster. Hoping to save his kingdom, Laomedon chained Hesione to some rocks near the sea and waited for the monster to arrive. Heracles, who was returning from fighting the Amazons, stopped off at Troy. Learning what was about to happen, Heracles killed the monster and requested Laomedon's immortal horses (which had been passed down from his grandfather Tros) as payment for rescuing his daughter. Laomedon agreed, but again he refused to pay. Heracles, angry at the Trojan king's broken promise, planned to return with an army, after he finished performing the twelve labors.

Heracles raised an army in Tiryns, and together with Telamon of Salamis (son of Aeacus) they went to attack Troy. After capturing the city, Heracles killed Laomedon, along with most of his sons. Victorious, Heracles gave Hesione to Telamon as his reward for helping win the war. However, Hercules allowed Hesione to ransom one captive of her choice. When her youngest brother Podarces was about to be sold into slavery, she ransomed him with her golden veil. Podarces later became king of Troy and changed his name to Priam, which means, "Ransom."

Hercules Rescues Hesione

#30a Priam, King of Troy

Priam was the last king of Troy. His reign, as well as his life, ended with the Trojan War. When his son abducted (or ran off with) Helen, wife of the Greek King Menelaus, the Greeks laid siege to the city of Troy, and stayed there for ten years.

Priam's queen was Hecuba, the daughter of a king (either King Dymas of Phrygia, or King Cisseus of Thrace… no one knows for sure… she could have been born of the river god Sangarius and Metope). Hecuba was rumored to have had a son named Troilus by the god Apollo. An oracle prophesied that Troy would not be destroyed if the boy should reach adulthood (age 20), but Achilles killed him, bringing to naught the prophecy. After the fall of Troy, Hecuba is said to have been enslaved by Odysseus.

Hecuba had a premonition of bad things to come and warned her son Hector not to fight Achilles, but Hector was bound by honor to take the fight unto himself, as his younger brother Paris was no match for the Greek warrior.

When Achilles killed Hector in single combat, he dragged Hector's body back to his camp and didn't respect it. Zeus sent Hermes to escort King Priam to the Greek camp. There Priam pleaded with Achilles to take pity on a grieving father and return Hector's body. He said, "I have endured what no one on earth has ever done before – I put my lips to the hands of the man who killed my son." Achilles was so moved that he returned Hector's corpse to the Trojans. Both sides agreed to a temporary truce, and Priam held a proper funeral for his son, complete with funerary games.

Priam and Hecuba's two daughters, Creusa and Troan, concern us further; the one would marry Aeneas; the other, Memnon.

King Priam was about 80 years old when Neoptolemus (Pyrrhus), son of Achilles, killed him. During the sack of Troy, Neoptolemus killed Priam's son Polites as he sought refuge on the altar of Zeus. Priam threw a spear at him, but it hit his shield and didn't harm him. Then Neoptolemus dragged old Priam to the altar and killed him there, too.

Priam Visits Achilles

#30b Tithonus of Troy

Tithonus was Priam's half-brother; his father was Laomedon, and his mother was named Placia. He was born in 1304 BC and died in 1237 BC. Somehow he escaped the wrath of Hercules when he was killing off Laomedon's sons.

Eos (Aurora), the goddess of the Dawn, was at times inspired with the love of mortals, just like her sister Selene (or Artemis), goddess of the Moon. Her favorite was Tithonus. One day she stole him away and persuaded Zeus to grant him immortality, but she forgot to include the gift of eternal youth in her request. Little by little she realized that he was growing old. When his hair was quite white, she cast him aside, but let him have free range of her palace, where he lived on ambrosial food and wore celestial clothes. Sadly, over time, he lost control of his limbs. Then she shut him up in his chamber, out of which his feeble voice might at times be heard. Finally, she turned him into a grasshopper.

Tithonus and Eos

#31 Memnon of Troy

Memnon was the son of Aurora (Eos) and Tithonus. As he was born in Ethiopia, he became their king. He dwelt in the extreme east, on the shore of the Red Sea. He married his cousin Troana, daughter of King Priam, the High King of Troy, and Hecuba. Their son was named Thor.

When the Greek-Trojan war broke out, Memnon came with his warriors to assist the kindred of his father. King Priam received him with great honors, and listened to his tale of the wonders of the ocean shore.

The very day after his arrival, Memnon led his troops to the field. He killed Antilochus, the son of Nestor, and put the Greeks to flight, but Achilles appeared and restored the battle. A long and uncertain contest ensued between Achilles and Memnon. Finally Achilles proved victorious, Memnon fell, and the Trojans fled in disarray.

Aurora viewed the danger of her son from her station in the sky. When she saw him fall, she directed his "brothers," the Winds, to convey his body to the banks of the river Esepus in Paphlagonia. In the evening Aurora came, accompanied by the Hours and the Pleiades, and wept and lamented over her son. Night, in sympathy with her grief, spread the heaven with clouds; all nature mourned for the fallen son of the Dawn.

The Ethiopians raised his tomb on the banks of the stream in the grove of the Nymphs, and Zeus caused the sparks and cinders of his funeral pyre to turn into birds which, dividing themselves into two flocks, fought over the pyre till they fell into its flame. Every year at the anniversary of his death they return and celebrate his funeral rites in like manner. To this day, Aurora remains inconsolable for the loss of her son. Her tears still flow— they may be seen at early morning in the form of dewdrops on the summer grass.

Departure of Memnon for Troy

#32 Thor of Thrace

Thor was the son of Priam's daughter Troana and Tithonus' son Memnon. He was born in Asgard (which in the *Prose Edda* simply means "Asian City," or Troy, or possibly Scythia). Thor was fair to look at with hair fairer than gold. After his father was killed, Thor was taken in by a certain duke called Lóríkus in Thrace. When he was twelve winters old, he had attained his full measure of strength – he was so strong he could lift 10 bear skins at once. Eventually he killed is foster father and mother (Lora) and took over the kingdom of Thrace.

Thor then travelled the earth, killing the frost giant Hrungnir (he rode into battle on a chariot pulled by goats), the Midgard Serpent, and many beasts. He met his wife, a prophetess named Sibyl (Sif) in the north. The legend of Thor and his hammer is well-known, but why would he carry a hammer as a weapon? Men in those days usually carried a battle-axe (and sometimes referred to their headstrong wives with a similar epithet). It is my guess that Thor's "hammer" was none other than his wife Sif, whose name sounds very, *very* similar to the Greek word for "hammer" – *sifuri* (σφυρί). The mythical name of his hammer, Mjolnir, means "flour." Perhaps she was his "flour maiden," or the person who baked bread for him. The myth is well-developed:

One night, Loki decided to cut off Sif's golden hair. When Thor caught up with him, he threatened to break every bone in his body. Loki promised to replace the golden hair with hair of real gold. Then the Trickster went to see the sons of Ivaldi, who were dwarves. They made a wig of finely spun gold, which had a magical property that made it come alive, like real hair. Woven into this tale is the story of how other dwarves had forged the hammer Mjolnir. It was foretold that during the end-of-the-world battle called Ragnarok, Thor would do battle with a great serpent and slay the beast, thanks to this hammer, but after taking nine steps, he would die of its venom.

The *Prose Edda* gives details concerning Thor's offspring: "In the northern part of the world he (Thor) met with and married a prophetess called Sibyl… Loridi, who resembled his father, was their son. Loridi's son was Einridi, his son Vingethor, his son Vingener, his son Modi, his son Magi, his son Sceaf (#39), his son Bedwig, his son Athra, his son Itermon, his son Heremod, his son Skjold, his son Beaw, his son Geata, his son Godwulf, his son Finn, his son Friallaf; he had a son named Woden, whom we call Odin (#55)… His (Odin's) wife was called Frigg or Freya."

Sibil, or Sif

Part 3
The Scandinavians

Tracing our ancestry back in time, it seems that all roads lead back to Odin. (Even Ragnar Lothbrok, as seen on TV, claimed to be a descendant of Odin.) Surely this Norse god made a great impact on Scandinavian society – he can probably lay claim to being the father of half of Europe. He even has a day of the week named after him in English – Wednesday (it's Anything Can Happen Day)! Was Odin a real person? If so, who was Odin?

In this section we will examine the descendants of Thor, who was born in Asgard, or Troy, the Asian City. Because Odin ventured northwards, eventually settling with his many sons in different parts of Northern Europe and Scandinavia, we no longer consider them "Trojans" — they are now known as Scandinavians. For now, let us focus on the original Scandinavians, beginning with Odin.

Yggdrasil, the World Tree

#55 Odin

The *Prose Edda* was written about AD 1220 by Snorri Sturluson, but Snorri left out half a dozen of Odin's ancestors. To set matters straight, Odin's father was Frithuwald Bor (#54), son of Frealaf (#53), son of Frithuwulf (#52), whose father was Finn (#51), whose father was Flocwald (#50), son of Godwulf (#49), whose father was Geata (#48), whose father was Taetwa Tecti (#47), son of Beaw (#46), whose father was Skjold (#45), son of Heremod (#44), whose father was Itermon (#43), whose father was (H)athra (#42), son of Hwala (#41), whose father was Bedwig (#40), whose father was Sceaf (#39), son of Magi (#38), whose father was Modi (#37), whose father was Vingener (#36), son of Vingethor (#35), whose father was Einridi (#34), son of Loridi (#33), whose father was Thor (#32), and whose mother was Sibyl.

Odin's descent from the house of Troy is significant. As we have seen before, the royal line of Troy was descended from Judah's son Zerah. Although in Old Norse Odin's name (*Othr*) means "ecstasy, inspiration, furor," W.M.H. Milner (1902) claims that "his name is Hebrew—*Aud'n* or *Odn* (for the broad A in the Hebrew carries often the sound of O), meaning Lord—human or divine" (*The Royal House of Britain*, p. 32).

Odin was born in Asgard (i.e., Troy, or Scythia) in 215 AD. His father was Frithuwald, his mother was Beltsea. When he was 22 years old, he married a daughter of Cadwalladr named Frigg. Both had the gift of prophecy.

At that time the Romans were busy subjecting all their neighbors to Roman rule. Rather than fight, Odin left his home in Scythia accompanied by a great number of men and women, both old and young. They passed through Russia, Germany and Denmark, finally settling in Sweden. Odin placed Germany under the rule of one of his sons, Vegdev. He placed Denmark under the rule of Skjold. He gave Norway to Saeming, a son of his second wife Skadi.

The plains and natural resources in Sweden appealed to Odin, so there he chose for himself a townsite now called Sigtuna. He appointed chieftains after the pattern of Troy, establishing twelve rulers to administer the laws of the land, and he drew up a code of laws like that which had been established in Troy and which the Trojans had followed. He kept his son Yngve with him, eventually passing the kingdom of Sweden to him.

Odin

Runes

Odin seemed to hunger and thirst for knowledge. In his quest for knowledge, Odin traveled to the roots of *Yggdrasil* (the World Tree) to try to access the Well of Higher Wisdom. There he was met by the guardian of the well, a giant called Mimir. Mimir told him that to receive a drink from the Well, he would need to sacrifice something that meant a lot to him. Therefore Odin cut out his eye and handed it to the giant. Mimir granted Odin his drink, which gave him the gift of insight into the past, present and the future.

"Knowledge is power" could be Odin's motto. Ever aware that knowledge could be passed from one generation to the next by means of writing, he sought a way to convey his knowledge to others. Once again he traveled to *Yggdrasil*, in order to make the Tree reveal Runes from its trunk (these were secrets carved by the Norns, or the three Fates, who lived in a well under the Tree). Once again Odin made a sacrifice, this time by hanging himself from the Tree for nine days and nine nights, during which he pierced himself with the spear Gungnir. (Notice how this tale echoes the story of Christ on the Cross.) At the end of his ordeal, the Runes spelled themselves out for Odin, who learned how to read them. In this experience Odin learned the the Runes are not only an alphabet, but also symbolic representations of the forces that structure the universe. (The word "rune" means not only letter, but also secret / mystery.)

Afterwards, Odin kept four animals with him: two ravens and two wolves, to tell him everything that was happening in the Nine Worlds. Even then, he realized that magic and wisdom were not enough to be powerful in the world. They must be communicated to others. With this intent, he set out to drink the Mead of Poetry. He shape-shifted into a serpent to get into the cave where it was held, then he shape-shifted into a handsome young man to deceive the maiden who guarded it. Then he shape-shifted into an eagle to escape.

The earlies Runes were from about 150 AD. The strokes are angular, meant to be carved in wood or stone; there are no horizontal marks. Although spoken language made a difference between long and short vowels, Runes did not (as English does not, today). Odin liked to use Runes to perform magic. For example, he used one to bring the dead back to life: "If I see up in a tree, a dangling corpse in a noose, I can so carve and color the runes, that the man walks and talks with me."

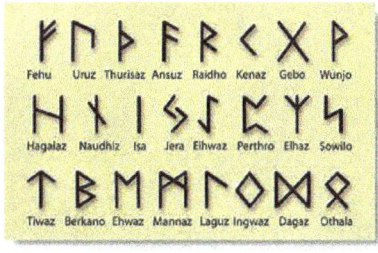

Runes

(#55) Frigg

Odin was known as the All-Father, whose wife Frigg sat by his side. Frigg was a *volva*, a kind of witch who practiced Norse magic (*seidr*). By this magic, she could discern someone's fate and work within its structure to bring about change, symbolically weaving new events into being. (In contemporary Latin culture, Clotho spun the thread of life, Lachesis wove it, and Atropos cut it off.)

Frigg owned falcon feathers that she used for shapeshifting. Like other Eurasian shamans, she was exalted, feared, longed for, celebrated, and scorned. Her role in the war council was to foretell the outcome of a suggested plan of action by means of divination, and to influence that outcome by active magic. She was like Wealtheow in *Beowulf*, serving ritual liquor and acting as an oracle.

It seems that Odin might have had several wives at different times, or perhaps all together at the same time. Odin was married to Frigg, to Freyja, to Gulveig, the sorceress who had a love for gold and was thrown into a fire for her desires only to be reborn three times, and to Jord. It has been argued that Frigg, Freyja, and Gulveig may have been the same woman with different names, each one had slightly different qualities that made them stand apart. One person whom Odin did not marry was Rinder the Frost Giant, but he had relations with her.

Of Odin's offspring, his children with Frigg were Balder, Hodor the blind archer, and Hermod the brave. Their beloved Balder was accidentally killed by their blind elder son Hodor, to which Hermod, their youngest and bravest, was sent to retrieve Balder's body in the underworld. He failed, as Frigg could not get the world to cry to bring him back. Inevitably, Hodor was killed by Vali, the illegitimate son of Odin who was conceived by the rape of his mother Rinder.

The word for "Friday" is named after Frigg, or her mythical counterpart Freya. However confusion should be avoided: Freya is a title, much like the German "frau," while Frigg means "beloved."

Frigg was probably the mother of Yngvi (#56), but it is hard to tell. Anyway, Yngvi married Friege Frea (196-214), and their son was called Njord.

Frigg

#57 Njord Swedes

A girl named Idun was the keeper of the *epli*, the fruits eaten by Odin and his friends to keep their youthful appearance. True apples were unknown in Scandinavia before the arrival of the Christians, so *epli* were probably some kind of berries or nuts.

One day Odin and Loki were out hiking in the mountains. They couldn't find any food, so they whacked an ox that was grazing in a herd to have for their dinner. When they tried to barbecue the meat, it wouldn't cook. Then they heard a voice from a very large eagle, perched on a branch above. It said it had used magic to prevent the meat from cooking, but if they gave it as much as it wanted, it would let them cook the rest of it. They agreed, but the eagle ate all the best pieces.

This made Loki mad, so he smacked the eagle with the branch of a tree. The eagle grabbed the branch, however, and flew (with Loki all dangling down) high up in the sky. Then Loki found out that the eagle was really the frost giant Thjazi, who had shape-shifted. He made Loki swear to bring him Idun and her golden fruits ("Eden's Apples").

Loki kidnapped Idun, but when their guardian of youth disappeared, Odin and his friends began to grow old and tired. They demanded that Loki bring her back. The rescue of Idun brought about the death of Thjazi the frost giant.

Thjazi had a daughter named Skadi. When she discovered her slain father, Skadi stormed into Odin's stronghold to seek revenge. Odin offered Skadi three tokens of compensation: Light, Laughter, and Love.

First, Odin took the eyes of the giant Thjazi and made them light up the sky. Then Loki managed to get Skadi to chuckle. Finally, Odin offered Skadi one his offspring as her husband. She chose her husband by the look of his legs and feet. Hoping to pick the legs and feet of Balder, she chose the seafarer Njord instead. However, they couldn't agree on where to live.

They tried living at Thrymheim (Thunder Mountain), which was Skadi's home. After the first nine nights, Njord could not tolerate the howling sound of the wolves and the coldness on the highest mountain peak. They spent the next nine nights in the home of Njord. This time it was Skadi that could not stand the cries of the seabirds. So they separated, and Njord married Nerthus of Nortun.

The Abduction of Idun

#58 Yngvi Frey

Yngvi Frey was born about 235 AD in Uppsala. Both Njord and his son Yngvi Frey were worshipped as gods by those who came after them. It was said that Frey ruled the rain and the sunshine, and had the power over the growth from the ground. He also ruled over men's fortune in property. He raised a large temple at Upaslir, which was the old name of Uppsala.

In the days of Frey the Peace of Frodi begaan. The people of Sweden became wealthier than before.

Frey married Gerd Gymersdottir, a giantess. Her name means "fence." Their descendants were known as the Ynglingar. Gerd was the most shiningly beautiful of all creatures, the spirit and image of soil fertility. (Her brother Beli was the leader of the Barking Giants.) Gerd at first rejected the proposal of marriage to Frey, even after his messenger Skirnir brought her eleven golden apples and a magic ring called Draupnir. Finally Skirnir threatened to use Frey's sword to cover the earth in ice (which would make her life rather sad and miserable), so she agreed to marry him. Nine days later, she met Yngvi Frey in a wood and married him. Their son was named Fjolnir.

Draupnir was forged by two dwarves, Brokkr and Sindri, who also made Thor's hammer. (Loki lost the wager, which might have cost him his head, but he argued that to chop off his head they would have to injure his neck, which was not part of the deal). Odin place this ring on the funeral pyre of his son Balder. Every nine nights the ring produced eight more gold rings of equal weight. It was later retrieved by Hermodor and offered as a gift to Gerd.

Then one day Yngvi Frey fell sick, and he took counsel and allowed a few men to see him. They made a large mound for him with a door and three holes. When he died, they carried him secretly into the mound and told all the countrymen that he was alive. They kept him there for three winters, and poured all the tax money into the mound – the gold through one hole, the silver through another hole, and the brass pennies through the third. In this way the peace and good seasons were coerced into continuing, even though Yngvi Frey was already dead.

The Temple at Uppsala

#59 Fjolnir Yngvi Freysson

Fjolnir, whose name means "much-knowing," was born in Uppsala. His name has also been interpreted as "concealer of the mead of poetry," which is a bit ironic, owing to the manner of his death. Odin himself used the name Fjolnir as one of his pseudonyms.

Fjolnir was said to have been a contemporary of Caesar Augustus (63 BC – 14 AD). However, most sources say he lived from 256-312 AD. Fjolnir's reign was a time of peace and prosperity.

When Fjolnir went to visit his friend Frodi, who ruled in Zealand, a great feast was prepared for him, and people were invited from far and wide. Frodi had a large hall, in which was a large vat, many feet high, held together by large timbers. It stood on the ground floor. There was a loft above it, in which liquid could be poured in through an opening. The vat was full of mixed mead, a very strong drink. In the evening, Fjolnir and his men slept in the room on the loft, above the vat. During the night Fjolnir went out on the balcony to look for the restroom. He was dead-drunk and so sleepy he could barely walk. On the way back to his room he walked along the balcony, and there he missed his footing and fell into the mead-vat and perished.

The name of his wife was not known, but they had one son: Svegdi.

#60 Svegdi Fjolnarsson

Svegdi, whose name means "waving one," was born in about 277 in Uppsala, then took the realm when his father died. He made a vow to search for Odin and Godheim (the land of the gods). He went far and wide with twelve men, came to Turkland, and was five winters on that journey. He married a woman called Vana in Vanaheim (one of the nine worlds that were situated around the tree Yggdrasil, in Sweden; the other eight were Asgard, Álfheimr, Midgard, Jötunheimr, Svartálfaheimr, Niflheim, Múspellsheimr, and Niðavellir). Their son was called Vanlandi.

After a while, Svegdi went again in search of Godheim. In the eastern part of Sweden (actually, Russia) there is a large stone called Stein, which stands as large as a big house. One evening after sunset, when Svegdi finished drinking and went to his sleeping-house, he saw a dwarf sitting outside on the rock. The dwarf stood in the door and shouted to Svegdi to come in if he wanted to meet Odin. Svegdi rushed into the rock which at once closed upon him, and he never came back.

Svegdi is Lured by a Dwarf

61 Vanlandi Svegdasson

Vanlandi, whose name means "Man from the Land of the Vanir," was born in Sweden in 298 AD. He was a great warrior and inherited the crown from his father Svegdi.

Vanlandi spent a winter in Finland with Snjae the Old, after which he married Snjae's daughter Driva. When spring came Vanlandi returned home; meanwhile, Driva gave birth to their son Visbur.

Developing a case of wanderlust, Vanlandi set off on a trip and promised to return in three winters, but did not do so. After ten winters, Driva schemed with the witch Huld either to bind Vanlandi to Finland or to kill him. During this time Vanlandi, who was in Uppsala, had a great desire to return to Finland, but his friends urged him not to do so. He did not return to Finland, so he was smothered by a demon (a "mara," in Norwegian) in his sleep and died. The Swedes took his body to a river called Skytaa and buried him there.

#62 Visbur Vanlandasson

Visbur, Vanlandi's son, was born in Sweden in 319 AD. He married the daughter of Aude the Rich, giving her three large farms and a gold ornament as wedding gifts. They had three sons, named Gisle, Ond and Domaldi. However, Visbur left her and married the daughter of Herleiv Frodeson (granddaughter of Frodi, King of the Danes), so she went home to live with her father Aude.

When Gisle and Ond (aged 12 and 13) sought revenge on their father for rejecting their mother and denying them their heritage, they did witchcraft with the sorceress Huld. Then they came with some men in the middle of the night, and burned Visbur in his hall.

Visbur's other son Domaldi ran into bad luck when his stepmother used witchcraft against him.

#63 Domaldi Visbursson

Domaldi, whose name means "Power to Judge," was born in Sweden in 340 AD. He married the daughter of Hoddbrodd Sverdhjaltsson; their son was named Domarr.

During his reign in Svitjod (Sweden) there was a famine. The Swedes arranged a huge sacrifice at Uppsala. The first year they sacrificed oxen, and when that did not work, the following year they sacrificed humans. When that did not work, the tribal leaders decided that Domaldi himself should be sacrificed. Therefore Dómaldi, was sacrificed by the Swedes to the goddess Ceres to ensure the fertility of the crops.

#64 Domar Domaldasson

Domar was born in 361 AD. He had better luck with the harvests and ruled for a long time in peace and prosperity. He married Drott, daughter of Dan the Arrogant, who gave his name to the Danes, and their son was named Dyggvi. Dómarr died in bed of sickness in Sweden. He was burned and buried at Uppsala.

#65 Dyggvi I Domarsson

Dyggvi, who was born in Sweden in 382 AD, also ended his life in that country. He died in bed, so he never reached Valhalla. Instead he went to Hel (the name of Loki's daughter), whose concubine he became. Ironically, his name means "Useful, Effective."

#66 Dag (the Wise) Dyggvasson

Dag was born in Sweden in 403 AD. He became the tenth king of the Yngling Dynasty. He was so wise that he understood the language of birds. He had a sparrow which flew to different countries and reported what it saw there. Once the sparrow flew to a farm called Varva in Gotland, taking the grain from a peasant's corn field. The peasant took a stone and killed the sparrow. King Dag was aggrieved that the sparrow did not come home. He made a sacrifice and inquired after the sparrow, and learned that it was killed at Varva. Then he assembled a great army and went to Gotland. When he landed with his men, they plundered Varva, and the people fled before him.

King Dag returned to his ships in the evening, after having killed many people and taken many prisoners. As they were going across a river, a slave laborer came running up to the riverside and threw a pitchfork into their troop. It struck the king on the head, so that he fell instantly from his horse and died.

King Dag Avenges His Sparrow

#67 Agni (the Powerful) Dagsson

Agni was born in Sweden in 424 AD. When his father Dag died in 440, Agni became king. One summer, he went to pillage Finland with his army. The Finns gathered a huge army against him, under a chief named Frosti. Agni won this great battle, and many Finns were killed together with Frosti. Agni then subdued all of Finland with his army. He captured not only great treasure, but also Frosti's daughter Skjalf and her brother Logi.

Agni returned to Stockholm and put up his tent on the side of the river where it is flat. There he married Skjalf, who became pregnant with two sons, Erik and Alrik. Skjalf asked him to honour her dead father Frosti with a grand feast, which he granted. He invited a large number of guests, who gladly attended. They had a drinking competition in which Agni became very drunk. Skjalf saw an opportunity and cooked up a plan.

The king's tent was next to the woods, under the branches of a tall tree. When Agne was fast asleep, Skjalf took a rope, had her men remove the tent, and threw the rope over a bough. Then she told her men to pull the rope and they hanged Agni, avenging Skjalf's father. Skjalf and her men ran to the ships and escaped to Finland, leaving her sons behind.

Agni was buried at that very place, which is presently called Agnafit, which is east of the Tauren (the Old Norse name for Södertörn) and west of Stockholm.

#68 Alrek (the Trembler) Agnisson

Alrek and his brother Erik became joint kings after the death of their father Agni. They were both powerful men, great warriors and sportsmen. They were experts at training horses to prance, gallop and race. One day while out riding on their best horses they failed to return. A party went out in search of them but found them both dead with crushed skulls. They had no weapons with them except the horses' bridles, so it was believed that they had killed each other with these.

Alrek married Dagreid, the daughter of King Dag, the Mighty. Their son was named Yngvi. They had another son named Alf.

Skjalf's Revenge

Alrek and Erik Fight a Duel

#69 Yngvi Alreksson

Yngvi was a great warrior king who always won his battles, the master of all exercises, happy, generous and sociable. His brother Alf was unsociable and harsh and stayed at home instead of pillaging other countries. Alf was married to Bera, who was happy and alert and a very lovable woman.

One day in autumn, Yngvi returned to Uppsala from a very successful raid. He loved to spend time at the drinking table until late at night, like his sister-in-law Bera, and they found it pleasant to talk to each other. Alf, however, preferred to go to bed early; he started to tell her to go to bed early as well so that she did not wake him. Then Bera would answer that Yngvi was much better for a woman than Alf, an answer that was getting on Alf's nerves.

One evening, the jealous Alf entered the hall and saw Yngvi and Bera talking on the high seat. The other guests were too drunk to see that Alf had arrived. Alf drew a sword from under his cloak and ran Yngvi through. Mortally wounded, Yngvi got up, drew his own short sword and slew Alf. They were buried in two mounds on the Fyris Wolds, near the Temple of Uppsala.

Alf and Yngvi Killing Each Other

#70 Jorund Yngvasson

Jorund, King Yngve's son, became king at Uppsala. He was often away in summer on war expeditions. One summer he went with his forces to Denmark; and having plundered all around in Jutland, he went into Lymfjord, and marauded there also. While he was camping in Oddesund with his people, a pirate named Gylog, son of King Gudlog of Halogaland, came up with a great force and challenged him to do battle. When the country people saw this they swarmed from all parts of the land, in great ships and small, and Jorund was overpowered by the multitude. He couldn't fight his way out of the fjord, which was about 140 miles long, so his ships cleared of their men. He sprang over-board, but was made prisoner and taken to the land. Gylog ordered a gallows to be erected, led Jorund to it and had him hanged there.

#71 Aun (The Aged) Jorundsson

Aun the Old (the same name as the Anglo-Saxon name Edwin), was born in 509 AD. He was a wise king who sacrificed greatly to the gods, but he was not warlike and preferred to live in peace. As a result, he was attacked by the Danish prince Halfdan (the grandson of Dan the Arrogant, the founder of Denmark). Aun lost the battle and fled to Geats, where he stayed for 25 years until Halfdan died in his bed and was buried in a mound. King Aun was then able to return to Uppsala, but by that time he was 60 years old. In order to live longer he sacrificed one of his own sons to Odin, who said that he would live as long as he sacrificed a son every ten years.

When Aun had sacrificed a son for the seventh time, he was so old that he could not walk but had to be carried on a chair. When he had sacrificed a son for the eighth time, he could no longer get out of his bed. When he had sacrificed his ninth son, he was so old that he had to feed by suckling milk from a horn like a little child.

After ten years he wished to sacrifice his tenth and last son. However, the Swedes refused to allow him this sacrifice, and so he died. He was buried in a mound at Uppsala and succeeded by his last son Egil. From that day, dying in bed of old age was called Aun's sickness among the Scandinavians.

Aun the Aged

#72 Egil Aunsson

Egil was born in 530 AD. He was no warrior, but sat quietly at home. When his father died, Egil inherited a slave named Tunni. This slave had been the counselor and treasurer of the king, and when Aun died, Tunni took a lot of treasure and buried it in the earth.

Now when Egil became king he put Tunni in among the other slaves. Together they ran away and dug up the treasures which Tunni had hidden. Afterwards many malefactors flocked to him, and they became outcast bandits. King Egil heard went out with his forces to pursue them, but one night when he had taken up his night quarters, Tunni came with his men, fell on the king's men, and killed many of them. As soon as King Egil perceived the commotion, he prepared for defense and set up his banner, but many people deserted him. King Egil saw that nothing was left to do but flee.

Then King Egil went to Sealand in Denmark, to Frode the Bold, and promised him tribute from the Swedes to obtain help. Frode gave him an army, and also his champions, with which force King Egil returned to Sweden. When Tunni heard this he came out to meet him, and there was a great battle in which Tunni was killed. King Egil recovered his kingdom, and the Danes returned home. King Egil sent King Frode great and good presents every year, but he paid no tribute to the Danes. However, the friendship between Egil and Frode continued without interruption.

It happened in Sweden that an old bull, which was destined for sacrifice, was fed so much that he became dangerous, and when they were going to lay hold of him he escaped into the woods. This bull became furious, and stayed in the forest wreaking great damage on the country.

King Egil was a skilled hunter and often rode into the forest to chase wild animals. Once he was out hunting with his men. The king tracked an animal for a long time and followed it in the forest, but he got separated from all his men. He observed at last that the animal he was tracking was the bull, so he rode up to it to kill it. The bull turned round suddenly, and the king struck him with his spear, but the bull tore itself out from the spear. The bull now struck his horn in the side of the horse, so that he instantly fell flat on the earth with the king. The king sprang up and tried to draw his sword, but the bull struck his horns right into the king's breast. The king's men then came up and killed the bull. The king lived but a short time, and was buried in a mound at Upsal.

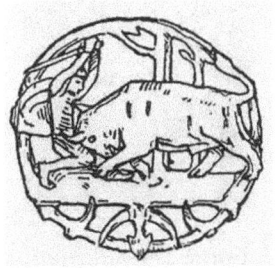

Egil and the Bull

#73 Ottar Egilsson

Ottar was born in Uppsala in 551 AD. When he became king, Ottar did not continue to be friendly with King Frode of Denmark. Therefore the Danish king sent messengers to King Ottar to demand the tribute which his father Egil had promised him. Ottar replied that the Swedes had never paid tribute to the Danes, and neither would he.

Now Frode was a great warrior, so he came to Sweden one summer with his army, and ravaged the country. He killed many people, took some prisoners, burned all the inhabited parts, took a great booty, and laid waste to the land. The next summer King Frode made an expedition to the eastward, and when King Ottar heard that Frode was not at home in his own country, he went on board his own ships, sailed over to Denmark, and ravaged there unopposed. As he heard that a great many people were collected at Zealand, he proceeded westward to the Sound, and sailed north to Jutland, and made desolate the country with his army.

The names of the earls whom Frode had appointed to defend Denmark while he was abroad were Vatt and Faste. When these earls heard what the Swedish king was doing, they collected an army, came unexpectedly upon Ottar, and immediately began a battle. The Swedes put up a good fight, and many people fell on both sides. But as soon as men fell in the Danish army, other men hastened from the country to replace them, and also all the nearby ships joined them. The battle ended with the fall of Ottar and the greater part of his people. The Danes took his body, carried it onto the land, laid it upon a mound of earth, and let the wild beasts and ravens tear it to pieces.

Thereafter they made a figure of a crow out of wood, sent it to Sweden, and told them that their king Ottar was no better than a scarecrow. From this event he was called Ottar Vendelcrow.

Ottar Vendilkraka

#74 Adils Ottarsson

Adils was born in Uppsala in 572 AD. His mother was the daughter of Eysten Frothisson of Denmark. For several summers, he went on Viking expeditions. On one of these trips he came to Saxland. The king of Saxland was called Geirthjof, and his wife was called Alof, but Adils knew nothing of their children. As it happened, the king was not at home, so Adils and his men plundered the king's house, while others drove a herd of cattle down to the strand. The herd was attended by slaves, churls, and girls, and they took all the people together with the cows. Among them was a remarkably beautiful girl called Yrsa. She was not one of the slave girls, and it was soon observed that she was intelligent, spoke well, and in all respects very well behaved. At last it came to to pass that that the king celebrated his wedding with her, though she was seven years his senior, and Yrsa became queen of Sweden.

At that time King Halfdan's son Helgi ruled over Leidre. He came to Sweden with so great an army that King Adils saw no other way than to flee. King Helgi took Queen Yrsa prisoner, took her to wife, and had a son by her called Rolf Kraki. After three years, Queen Alof came to Denmark and told Queen Yrsa that she was her mother. Then Yrsa went back to Sweden to King Adils. King Helgi died in a battle, and eight-year-old Rolf Kraki became king in Leidre.

King Adils was a great lover of good horses and had the best horses of anyone. One of his horses was called Slongve, and another was called Raven. This horse he had taken from a king he had slain in battle, and Raven's foal was also called Raven. King Adils was at a sacrifice, and as he rode around the hall his horse Raven (II) stumbled and fell, and the king was thrown forward upon his head. His skull was split, and his brains were dashed out against a stone. Adils died at Uppsala and was buried there in a mound.

Yrsa of Uppsala and Saxland

#75 Eystein Adilsson

During Eystein's lifetime (594-620), many sea kings ravaged the Swedish shores. King Eystein was at a feast in Lofond (Lovon), Malaren Lake, Sweden. Just then a sea-king called Solvi, a son of Hogni of Njardo, who was plundering in the Baltic, but had his dominion in Jutland, came with his forces to Sweden. Solvi came unexpectedly in the night on Eystein, surrounded the house in which the king was sleeping, and burned him and all his court. Solvi then went to the Swedes to try to get their approval. After an eleven-day battle (which he won), he became king, but finally the Swedes betrayed him and had him killed.

#76 Yngvar (The Tall) Eysteinsson

Yngvar, the son of Eystein, reclaimed the Swedish throne for the House of Yngling after the Swedes rebelled against Sölvi. He was a great warrior who often spent time patrolling the shores of his kingdom fighting Danes and pirates from the east. King Ingvar finally made peace with the Danes and dealt harshly with the Estonian pirates. Then he started pillaging Estonia in retribution, and one summer he arrived at a place called Stein (the Stone where a dwarf tricked #61, Svegdi Fjolnarsson). The Estonians assembled a great army and attacked King Ingvar. The Estonian forces were too powerful, Ingvar died, and the Swedish forces retreated. Ingvar was buried in a mound at a place called Stone Fort on the shores of Estonia.

#77 Skira Ingvarsson

Skira Ingvarsson (born in 620) is said to have descended from Gomer, son of Japheth, but that much is true of all the Scandinavians.* His first wife was Una Ingvarsson of Holmgard. His second wife was Aud Hilde Ivarsdottir of Denmark. Their son was Radbard of Gardgarige (Land of Farms).

* A possible alternative lineage, not including Skira: Eystein, Yngvar, Braut-Onundr, Ingjaldr, Olafr, Halfdan, Gudrod, Olaf II, Ragnvald, Ragnar Lothbrok.

#78 Radbard, King of Gardarige

Radbard, who was born in Russia in 638, married the fugitive princess Auður the Deep-Minded without the consent of her father, King Ivar "Wide Fathom" Halfdansson of Scane, who soon set out to punish his daughter. It was her 2nd marriage. Her lover, Helgi the Viking, was killed by her first husband Rurik, who then was killed by her father. However, King Ivar died on his way back home (his boat sank, and he drowned in the icy waters of the Gulf of Finland).

Auður took her child from her second marriage, Harald "Wartooth" Hraereksson, and left for the Swedish settlements in Russia. There she married King Radbard. And so Radbard helped Auður's son Harald Wartooth claim his maternal grandfather's (Halfdan Frodasson's) possessions in Sweden and Denmark.

#79 Randver Radbardsson of Lethra

Randver, born in 670, was the son of Radbard and Auður, the daughter of King Ivar Vidfamne (Wide Fathom) and Queen Gauthild Alfsdottir. Randver was married first to Ingild, the daughter of an unknown Swedish king. He later married Asa, Princess of Norway, the daughter of Harold Red Lips, King of Adgar. He was succeeded by his son Sigurd Ring, whose mother was (quite possibly his namesake) Randver's third wife, Signy of Essex, whose mother was Saint Osgyth of Mercia (see below, page 45).

#80 Sigurd "Ring" Randversson

Whether his mother was Signy of Essex or Asa Haraldsdottir of Norway makes little difference. Sigurd was born in Sweden in 730 AD.

Harald Wartooth had inherited Sweden from his grandfather Ivar Wide Fathom (see #79, above), but he ruled Denmark and East Goatland. His subordinate, Sigurd Ring, ruled Sweden and West Goatland. Harald realized he might die of old age and therefore not go to Valhalla, so he asked Sigurd if he may engage in battle and die gloriously. Both prepared for seven years and raised armies of about 200,000 each, as well as 300 shieldmaidens. The Swedes chopped down entire forests and built 3,000 ships to carry them over to the battlefield, which was Bravalla, in East Goatland. After a great many heroic feats by both champions and shieldmaidens, Harald's steward (named Bruni) decided his king had gained enough glory, so he crushed his skull with a club. More than 40,000 warriors had died, but Sigurd "won" the battle and became king of all Sweden and Denmark.

Sigurd married Alfhild, the daughter of Gandolf Asgeirsson, Count of Alfheim. In the old sources, he is notable for being the father of Ragnar Lodbrok.

#81 Ragnar "Lodbrok" Sigurdsson

Sigurd the Dragonslayer and Brynhild the Valkyrie had a daughter named Aslaug. Orphaned at the age of three, little Aslaug was taken in by a poor family in Norway, who nicknamed her Kraka (the Crow) to keep her true identity a secret.

Ragnar, son of King Sigurd Ring of Denmark, went to help the Jarl of Gotaland, who had a "dragon" problem. A snake had grown too big for its britches and was terrorizing the town. He boiled his cloak in pitch, put on hairy breeches to protect his legs from the dragon's blood, and speared it to death. As a reward, he was given the Jarl's daughter Thora in marriage. They had two sons, named Eirek and Agnar. Thora fell ill and died, so Ragnar once again went raiding.

In Norway, Ragnar happened upon the farm where Kraka (Aslaug) lived and desired to marry her. Although Kráka told him she had been cursed to give birth to a son with no bones if her husband proved too impatient on her wedding night (he was supposed to wait three nights), Ragnar could not control himself.

Thus, Ivar the Boneless was born. Their other children include Bjorn Ironsides, Hvitserk, Ubba, Sigurd Snake-in-the-Eye and Rognvald.

After boasting that he would invade England with just two ships, Ragnar was captured by King Ælla of Northumbria and thrown into a snake-pit, where he died. Ragnar's sons then avenged their father by sailing to England and torturing Ælla by performing the blood-eagle on him (a form of torture by ripping open his back).

It was said that Ragnar may have had two other wives, Lagertha and Swanloga. As "Lothbrok" is a feminine form, it is possible that Lagertha was Loðbróka, a first wife who had placed a charm on him to protect him from the Serpent of Goatland.

Without the invention of a compass, Viking raids were for the most part limited to the seacoasts. It was Ragnar who found a way to navigate over the open sea, a discovery that led to the Viking raids at Lindisfarne, and the eventual colonization of England by the Scandinavians. Before we get to that, however, let us go backwards in time (after a brief interlude on the following page) to talk about another group of colonizers who took a different route, through Spain, and settled in Ireland.

Ragnar and Kraka

Saint Osgyth

Saint Osgyth was a princess of Mercia, in Britain. Her father was King Frithwald; her mother Wilburge herself was descended from the kings of the Mercians. As a small child, Osgyth was sent to be educated by her Aunt, Saint Edith, an abbess at a nunnery at Aylesbury.

One day Osgyth's aunt sent her on an errand to deliver a book to St. Modwenna. To reach Modwenna's house, she had to cross a bridge over a stream. It was a windy day, and the stream was swollen with floodwater. Just as she was about to cross, a great gust of wind blew Osgyth into the cold water. When she did not return, Edith was very upset and went to find Modwenna.

The two women searched the countryside. Three days later they found the child lying in the stream, tragically drowned. St. Modwenna prayed for Osgyth and commanded her to arise from the water and come to them, and miraculously, Osgyth obeyed.

This miracle changed Osgyth's life forever (wouldn't it change anybody?): she decided she wanted to become a nun. Her parents did not agree with this choice and betrothed her to Sighere, the King of Essex, in order to form an alliance.

However, while her husband was away hunting, Osgyth made her mind up to keep her vow and become a nun, no matter what. She would rather be an abbess than a queen.

At first her husband protested that without her, life held no happiness for him, but he relented when their daughter Signy was born. Finally, he granted her wish, generously giving her land upon which to build a nunnery and a church.

Here, Osgyth lived in peace as Abbess for a number of years. Then one sunny autumn day when she was walking in the woods, enjoying the beauty of nature, her peace was forever shattered.

A gang of Viking pirates had landed on the Essex coast, in eastern Britain. Osgyth came face to face with the Viking leader in a clearing in the woods, but bravely stood her ground. The pagan pirates had little respect for Christian beliefs or for the pleas of this abbess. Their leader beheaded Osgyth on the spot, with one single swing of his sharp, glinting weapon. Then the pirates moved on to destroy the nunnery.

This time there was no St. Modwenna to save the day and bring Osgyth back to life. However, legend tells how she bent down and picked up her own head, and guided by angels, she carried it in her hands to the nunnery church. She loudly struck the door once with her blood-stained hand to warn the nuns of the approaching peril, then fell on the ground and died.

At the place of her martyrdom, in the woods, a spring gushed forth. The spring became a stream, and a well was built there in her honor. This became known as St. Osgyth's sacred well. The waters were used to bless ill people, who often found themselves cured.

It must be a scary sight for travelers who are unfortunate enough to be in Nun's Wood after dark. At certain times of the year, it is said that the murdered abbess can be seen, head in hands, once again visiting the well, the wood, and the church where the brutal events took place.

Part 4
Vikings in Ireland

Between AD 700 and AD 1100, many Vikings left Scandinavia and traveled to Britain and Ireland. Some went to plunder treasure. Others settled in new lands as farmers. Many of these invasions centered on Eastern England, where they eventually established the Danelaw (Danish Law). Other settlements focused on Western Scotland (the Isles) and the southernmost part of Ireland. Dublin (*Dubh Linn* = Dark Pool) is located in central Ireland, on the east coast. Waterford is located on the southeast corner of the nation.

#82 Ivar "The Boneless," King of Dublin

Ivar the Boneless was born with a handicap, fulfilling the curse place on his mother Aslaug and his father Ragnar. In fact, his upper body seemed to have had an extraordinary strength, despite his lack of bones. He grew up alongside his siblings, probably in Sweden, and garnered a reputation for being as fierce and ruthless as his father. Ivar was by far the most intelligent son of Ragnar. As he was also the oldest, he naturally became their leader.

When Ragnar's sons sailed to England seeking revenge against King Ælla, Ivar the Boneless refused to fight (anyway, he would have to have been carried into battle on a stretcher or a shield). The brothers were defeated and went home. Ivar, however, stayed in England – he had hatched a cunning plan. Going to see Ælla and making the case that he had not joined the fight against him, Ælla agreed to compensate him for his father's death and would give him as much land as he could cover with the biggest bull-hide he could find. Ivar stretched a hide to its limits, cut it into thin strips and covered a much larger territory than King Ælla had imagined. Founding the city of York there, Ivar spent his time forging local connections before inviting his brothers to come back and exact their revenge on Ælla. With Ivar's new friends aiding them, and Ælla thinking Ivar was on his side, they defeated Ælla and tortured him. They cut an "eagle" in Ælla's back, then severed all his ribs from his backbone with a sword, in such a way that his lungs were pulled out. Ouch!

Ivar remained a local king in England for a long time after, ruling from York. He was also apparently a companion of Olaf the White, the Viking sea-king of Dublin. Irish sources claim that Ivar and Olaf ruled Dublin together and led their army to several battles in Ireland in the 850s. According to the Anglo-Saxon historian Æthelweard, Ivar passed away in 870. In 1686, a burial mound was found by a farm laborer at Repton in Derbyshire, England. More than 250 partial skeletons have been since discovered around the mound, implying that this was the final resting place of a man of very high status. Some scholars believe that this was Ivar. (Two hundred fifty is more than enough – I guess Ivar wasn't as "boneless" as some people make him out to be!)

It matters not whether Ivar the Boneless was able to bear children of his own, nor whether he was truly the son of Ragnar Lothbrok. Because he married Ragnar's daughter Ingiald, he was at least Ragnar's son-in-law, and Ragnar's bloodline was continued, regardless of who Guthorm's true father was.

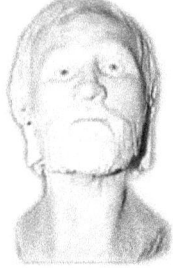

Ivar the Boneless

#83 Guthorm, King of Dublin

Guthorm was born around 835 in Northumberland and died about 890 in the Hebrides, Scotland. His father was Ivar the Boneless, and his mother was Ingiald Ragnarsdottir. The Vikings were expelled from Dublin in 902. Some went to France, some to England, and some to Wales. In 914, a large Viking fleet travelled to Waterford, in southern Ireland. He is also known as Gofraid, or in Irish, *ua imair*, meaning grandson of Imar (Ivar).

King Guthorm was married to the daughter of the Danish King Ragnar. He had four sons, one of whom was Ragnall mac Gofraid, who ruled Northumbria 934-944.

#84 Ranald, King of Dublin, Waterford & York

Ragnall came to prominence in 910, when he defeated the Danes of York and took control of that kingship. In 914, he crushed Barid son of Ottar in a naval engagement off the Isle of Man. That same year, he lent support to a new Scandinavian settlement at Loch Dá Cháech (Waterford harbor, in southern Ireland) and was soon recognized as ruler of the colony. When the settlers suffered two setbacks in engagements with the men of Munster, Ragnall took personal charge of their forces in the summer of 917. In August he led reinforcements northwards to Tipperary, where the king of Tara had already engaged with an advance Scandinavian party. A standoff enabled his brother Sitriuc Cáech to defeat the Leinstermen near the River Barrow and take control of Dublin. The following year Ragnall became king of York and defeated King Causantín II of Scotland at the second battle of Corbridge. He reached a *modus vivendi* with the Scots, which helped him in linking the political and commercial interests of Dublin and York.

Ragnall died in 921, apparently of natural causes.

#85 Ivar, Prince of Waterford

Ivar was born in 900 AD, the son of Ranald, King of Waterford, Dublin and York. He married Slani, a daughter of Brian Boruma, who descended directly from Milesius through his father King Cennetig, and indirectly, through his mother Be Bind, to King David of Israel. He died in 950 AD.

With Ivar's marriage to Slani, we are beginning to see a trend of hybridization, that is, the inter-marriage of Scandinavians with native Irish. With the eventual departure of the Scandinavians, these people will become true Irishmen and, as events unfold, true Scots.

Let's have a look at the ancestry of Slani (Table 5).

Table 5. The Ancestors of Slani ingen Brian

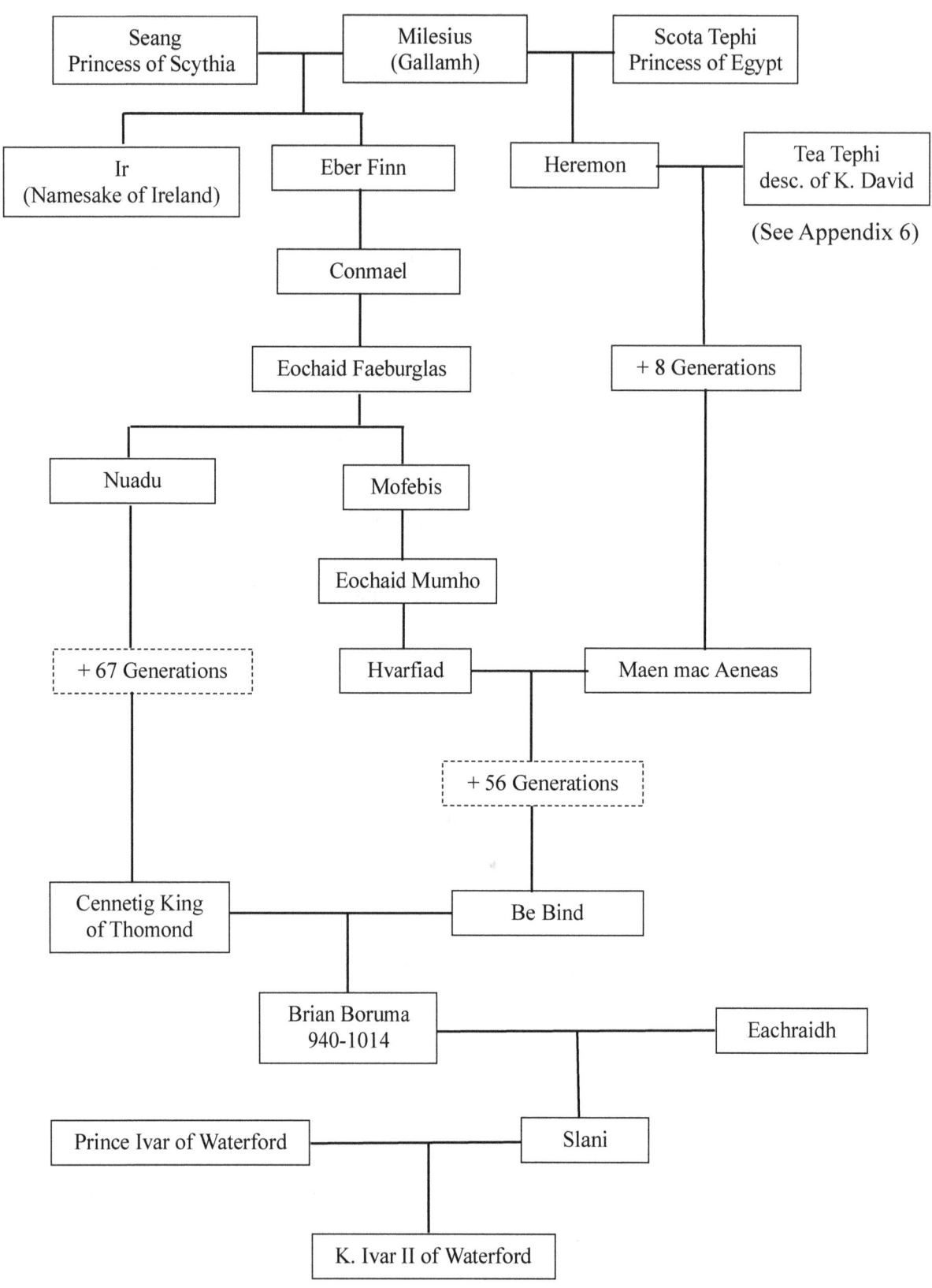

#86 King Ivar II of Waterford

Ivar belonged to the "Ui Imair" (Children of Imar) dynasty of Norse-Gaels who ruled over the Irish sea region, Dublin, and the western coast of Scotland, including the Hebrides.

We don't see much of Ivar before the 980s, but in 982 we know that he plundered Kildare. The next year Ivar joined forces with the King of Leinster in a battle against Mael Sechnaill (High King of Ireland), but his side suffered a great loss, including the death of his son Gilla Patraic. The following year (984) Ivar entered into an alliance with Brian Boruma (his maternal grandfather) to ravage the area, but they did not reach Dublin. Nine years later (993) he was expelled from Dublin by Silkbeard, "through the intercession of the saints" (after all, Ivar was still a pagan). Afterwards, another of Ivar's sons named Randolphe was killed by the men of Leinster. In 998 he attacked Leinster again, but his army lost most of their horses in that battle. During this time, he may have been involved in a number of raids in southwestern England, for he was the foremost Viking raider at the end of the Millennium.

One of his wives was the daughter of Donnuban mac Cathail (progenitor of the O'Donovan family). Another was a daughter (Aoife?) of Gilla Patraic mac Donnchada, King of Osraige and Ossory. His son and successor was Ragnall mac Imair.

Ivar and his family were involved in a hundred-year feud with the descendants (including Silkbeard) of Olaf Cuaran, King of Northumbria and Dublin (his name *cuaran* means "sandal" – I wonder if he word sandals?). This resulted in the loss of Dublin to the Irish O'Brien family, founded by Brian Boruma (Slani's father). Brian's descendants continued to rule Munster for two hundred years, at which time their territory shrank to become the Kingdom of Thomond.

Throughout the rule of the O'Brians, the system of tanistry was used to decide succession. In this system the Tanist is the heir-apparent, similar to the Prince of Wales in England today. Unlike the Prince of Wales, the Tanist was elected by the family as the most suitable male to become king, not necessarily the firstborn.

Ireland in 1014

#87 King Ranald I Ivarsson

This Ranald was born in Dublin in 974 AD. He was the son of Ivar II, King of Waterford and Dublin, who died in 1000.

#88 King Ranald II Ranaldsson

Ranald King of Waterford was born in Perth, Scotland, about 995, His father was Ragnvald Ivarsson, King of Waterford, and his mother was Radnall Ivarrsdottir.

He married Subneach (Suibine) Nic Niallghusa (great-granddaughter of Godfrey MacFergus) and had at least two sons (Echmarcach Meargach and Cacht) and two daughters. He was killed in 1035, in Dublin, Ireland, at the age of 60, and was buried there.

#89 Echmarcach Meargach MacRagnaill

Echmarcach mac Ragnaill, King of Dublin, Man and Galloway, was born in Ireland in 1010. His father was Ranald, King of Waterford, and his mother was Subneach Nic Niallghusa II, Queen of Waterford. He had at least one daughter and one son, but his wife's name remains unknown.

Meargach reigned as King of Dublin from 1036 to 1038, but he was forced out of Dublin by Diarmait mac Mael Nambo. He is one of three kings who submitted to Knut Sveinnson, ruler of the Anglo-Scandinavian Empire.

He died in Scotland in 1065 at the age of 55.

#90 Solam (Solomon, or Solmund)

Solom MacMeargaigh, King of Dublin, was born in 1000, in the Orkney Islands. He was the son of King Echmarcach mac Ragnaill, King of Dublin, Man and Galloway. He married Miss St. Columba (granddaughter of Godfrey MacFergus) sometime before 1060, in Argyll, Scotland.

Godfrey MacFergus had come to Scotland from Ireland in 836 to help King Kenneth McAlpin fight the Vikings. He served a short time as ruler of the Isles and eventually married Kenneth's sister. Godfrey died in 853.

Solam had at least one son, Giolla. He died in 1083 in the Hebrides, Scotland, at the age of 83, and was buried there.

#91 Giolla Adhamnan

Giolla Adhamnan was born in 1065 in Finlaggan Castle, Isle of Islay, Scotland. His father was Solam; his mother was Columba.

He married (first) Raginhild Olafsatter, (second) Ingeborg Skjolding, and (third) Thora ingen Godfrey MacFergus, Princess of Argyll (Oriel).

Increasingly threatened by the Norwegians, Gille took refuge in Ireland to seek military support. While there, his daughter married Harold Gillis (IV), King of Norway (1102-1136) in an attempt to bring peace.

#92 Gillebride MacGille Adomnan (Giolla Brighid)

GilleBride MacGille Adamnan was born in 1085, in Argyll, Scotland. (His name means "Servant of St. Brigid.") His father was King Giolla Adomnan Siol-Cuinn, King of Islay, and his mother was Thora ingen MacFergus na Oriel, grand-daughter of King Alpin. His father was forced to flee to Ireland by the violence of the Norwegians.

Gillebride returned to the coast of Scotland and took shelter in caves near Dunadd (the old center of Dalriadic rule) from which he fought the Vikings. He had persuaded some of his Irish kinsmen, the descendants of Colla, to help him. They made frequent attacks on their enemies, but their enemies were powerful and numerous. All the islands from Man to the Orkneys, and all the borderland, from Dumbarton to Caithness, were in the possession of the Norwegians, and those Gaels who remained were protecting themselves in the woods and mountains. In the end, Gille-Bride failed to retake his paternal lands. However he married a Viking woman (Berthoc Imergisdatter) and they had a son, Somerled, who was to become one of Scotland's greatest heroes and the progenitor of the Clan Donald and the Lords of the Isles.

In 1164, Gillebride died in Renfrewshire at the age of 84, and was buried in Scotland.

From this point we will interrupt our "saga" of the Vikings and go back in time to the beginnings of the Irish nation. As history progressed, the Vikings intermarried with the Irish, and the Irish began colonizing Scotland. The original Hebrew / Trojan / Scandinavian / Viking lineage picks up again with #93 Somerled MacGillebride (1115-1164, see page 91).

The Battle of Stamford Bridge

Shortly after Giolla was born, events unfolded on the other side of the British Isles, events which would shape the future of Scotland in profound ways. Godwin, the Earl of Wessex (d. 1052), had several sons who wielded enormous power: Harold, the new Earl of Wessex; Tostig, Earl of Northumbria; Gyrth, Earl of East Anglia; and Leofwine, Earl of Kent.

King Edward the Confessor of England died in 1066. (Edward had married Godwin's daughter Edith of Mercia.) The Witan (the King's Council) convened and selected Harold as the next king.

However, Duke William II of Normandy believed that King Edward had made a promise that he should be the next king.

Harald Hardrada, King of Norway, assembled three hundred ships to invade England. By his side was Tostig, who had been exiled by his brother Harold Godwinson in 1065.

Anticipating an attack from Normandy, Harold remained in Southern England. When he learned of the Norwegian invasion, he made haste to Yorkshire in four days. The Stamford Bridge crossed the Derwent River.

Before the battle, Harold rode up to Harald Hardrada and Tostig, offering to return Tostig's earldom if he would change sides. The offer was refused.

The English army, heavily armed, were held off by a giant Norseman on the bridge. This gave the lightly armed Norwegians, who were expecting only local opposition, to regroup. An English soldier floated under the bridge in a half-barrel and thrust his spear up through the wood to kill the giant axe-man. During the battle, Harald Hardrada took an arrow in his throat. Tostig was also killed. A second group of Norwegians that had been left to guard the ships mounted a second attack, but they too were defeated.

Weakened by this battle and exhausted from the long ride, King Harold was soon defeated, as Duke William II of Normandy landed three days after the battle on the south coast of England. In the Battle of Hastings, Harold was killed and William became King William I (the Conqueror).

Anglo-Saxon rule came to an end, and Norman rule began in England.

Part 5
Ireland

Legend has it that Bith, another one of Noah's sons who was refused entry to the Ark, built a ship of his own and fled to the furthest corner of the earth (as he thought), in the hopes that the waters of the coming Flood would somehow not reach him there. He took with him his daughter Cesaire (sounds like an airline company that flies Cesnas), his son Ladra the pilot, his nephew Fintan mac Bochra and fifty maidens. After her father and brother died, Cesaire and all the others were drowned in the Deluge. Fintan alone survived, taking the shapes of a salmon, an eagle, and a falcon. He witnessed the ages unfold, finally telling his tale before an assembly of sages in the late 6th century.

The second invasion took place under Partholon, a descendant of Magog. He defeated a North African pirate named Clapperleg and his monstrous Tuatha de Domnu, "Tribe of the Deep." After many generations the Partholonians were wiped out by the dog-head plague.

The third invasion was made by Nemed, a descendant of the Greeks of Scythia (descendants of Japheth, through Magog). He led a colony from the Caspian Sea to Ireland. The pirates (remember Clapperleg?) made his descendants pay an oppressive tribute from their stronghold on Tory Island.

During that time Fenius Farsaidh (#14) left his home in Scythia for the gathering of nations in Babylon. Fenius took advantage of the confusion of languages by opening a linguistics school on the Plain of Ibitena. Fenius' son Nel (#15), who was born at the Tower, went to Egypt where he was given an estate on the Red Sea, as well as Princess Scota for his bride (she was the same girl who had rescued baby Moses as he floated in a basket in the river). This was done in exchange for bringing his knowledge of languages to the service of Pharaoh. Nel's son Goedel (#16) later combined all the best features of the 72 languages, and the Irish tongue (Gaelic) was created.

As a child, Nel's son Goedel had been cured of a deadly snakebite by Moses, a bite which left the boy with a green mark where the snake had bitten (hence the epithet Goedel Glas, which means "green"). Moses prophesied that Goedel's descendants would live in a land free of serpents, and this came to pass, as there are no snakes native to Ireland. During the Exodus, when the Egyptians pursued the Hebrews, Nel hijacked the royal fleet and took it to sea. Pharaoh and his army drowned while pursuing the departing Hebrews. Afterwards, Nel and his family stayed in Egypt.

Two generations later, the new Pharaoh (Tuir, or Taa) sought revenge for Nel's refusal to join in the pursuit of Moses. Goedel's grandson Sruth (#18) had to escape, so again they stole Pharaoh's ships and sailed down the Red Sea to Sri Lanka and on to the River Indus. (This was plausible in the collapse of order triggered by the fall of Troy and the Sea Peoples' destruction of the Hittite and Mycenaean trade monopolies.) Then they crossed Central Asia to Scythia, on the shore of the Caspian Sea. There they became embroiled in a dynastic struggle. After five generations they sailed past the Caucasus to the Ukrainian Sea of Azov.

Meanwhile the Tuatha De Danann, Nemedians who had learned magic and witchcraft among the Greeks, used their magic to defeat the Fir Bolg, a tribe that had been enslaved and forced to carry earth in bags (the name *Fir Bolg* means "Dirt Bag").

After two hundred years, a Gael named Brath (#33) led an expedition across the Mediterranean to Spain. There he conquered the pirate city of Briganza. His son Breogan (#34) built a tower, from which his grandson Ithe chanced to see Ireland on a clear winter's night. Ithe traveled to Ireland, but the Danann killed him, fearing he would bring more invaders. His son escaped to report his murder to the sons of his cousin Milesius (#36) in Spain. These eight sons set out to avenge Ithe's murder, but five of them were lost in a storm at sea.

Up until that time, Ireland had been ruled by three brothers who took turns being king. During the year that the sons of Milesius landed and conquered it (1699 BC, the year following Solomon's construction of the Temple in Jerusalem), the country was ruled by King MacCuill, whose wife was named Eire. That is why the country was called Eire-land, after that king's wife.

Finally, the Gaels overcame the magic of the Tuatha De Danann with spells cast by their Druid priest Amergin (Miles himself used wax to block out the songs of the sirens, oddly reminiscent of Odysseus in Homer's *Odyssey*). They drove the rulers of Ireland underground, where they became fairies.

Milesius, by the way, had three lions on his shield. While on an expedition in Africa, he killed three lions in one morning. Thereafter each of his sons Heber and Heremon (Ir was not much of a fighter), and his grandson Heber Donn, bore a lion of a different color on his shield.

Scholars sometimes disagree as to the lineage of Irish kings, not to mention their chronological order. Before the arrival of the written word, oral genealogy was central to Irish culture. Every aspect of social privilege was derived from carefully counted descent from a Gaelic ancestor. Standard narratives were maintained by regularly scheduled recitals before critical conventions of scholars. The histories were highly esteemed, being narrated by professors who had spent twenty years learning them. Over the years, we have lost the oral tradition that was so important in early Ireland.

Beginning in the Middle Ages, we began to rely on the written word, which unfortunately was subject to the whims of a fledgling literate society. That is why we have a number of discrepancies regarding the lineage of our ancestors.

As time went on, mixed marriages took place, often in order to keep the peace. Thus the lines between Irish, Scots and Scandinavians began to blur. Let us begin with Queen Tea Tephi.

#51 Queen Tea Tephi / 37-m King Heremon

Tea Tephi was born in Spain. She married Heremon, one of the sons of Milesius. In the "Age of the World" 3500 (according to the *Annals of the Four Masters*) the sons of Milesius sailed to Ireland to take it from the Tuatha De Dananns. In the fight, Heremon, Emer, and Amergin slew the three jointly "rotating" kings macCeacht, macCuill, and macGreine, respectively. Their queens Eire, Fodhla, and Banba were also slain. Sadly, Milesius' widow Scota, daughter of the Egyptian Pharaoh, died in this battle, too. Heremon and Eber assumed joint sovereignty over Ireland. However, the following year they had a falling out and Eber was killed. Heremon took over as King of all Ireland.

Tea was the daughter of Lughaidh, a son of Milesius' uncle Ithe. When her time drew near, she requested a hill to be buried on. This became known as Teamhair. Heremon died 15 years later.

38-m Irial Faidh

Irial "The Prophet" Faith was the youngest son of Heremon and Tea. During his reign Irial cleared twelve plains and built seven forts, and cleared much of the country's ancient forests. He fought four battles against the Fomorian pirates. He died at Mug Maud around 1269 BC and was succeeded by his son Ethriel (39-m), who was not succeeded by his son, Follain (40-m), who was denied the monarchy by Conmaol, who killed his father.

41-m Tighernmas

Tighernmas, a great-great-grandson of Heremon and Tea, married Princess Sinusa, herself a great-great granddaughter of Lugaidh. He fought 27 battles against the kindred of Eber Finn, nearly eliminating the line.

Tighernmas first smelted gold in Ireland. He covered goblets and brooches with gold and silver and gave them to his followers. He also dyed clothes purple, blue and green cloth. At the end of 3656 (about 1544 BC), Tighernmas died along with 3/4 of the men of Ireland, while worshiping an idol. It happened precisely on the night of Samhein. Ireland went without a king for a seven years.

Then in 3644 Eochaidh Etgudach was chosen as king by the remaining quarter of men who did not die in idolatry. During his reign, clothes were dyed according to one's rank: one color was for slaves, two for soldiers, three for goodly heroes or young lords, six for ollavs (learned men), and seven for kings or queens. (This was possibly the origin of the Tartan plaid.) He was killed in battle at Tara. Thereafter thirty-nine generations ruled, until Conn of the Hundred Battles.

82-m Conn Ceadchathach (of 100 Battles)

Conn's father was Felim Rachtmar the Lawgiver; his mother was Ughna Ollchrothach, Princess of Denmark. The night he was born, five new roads were discovered, all leading to Tara.

There is a coronation stone called *Lia Fail* at Tara (that is, *Teamhair*), which is said to roar when the rightful king stands on it. When Conn stood on it, the stone roared for the first time since being split by Cuchulainn when it failed to roar for Lugaid Riab Derg. The stone had been half-buried since that time, but Conn accidentally stepped on it, making it roar. A druid was busy explaining the meaning to Conn, when a magical mist arose. A horseman approached and threw three spears towards Conn, then asked Conn and the druid to follow him to his house. The house stood on a plain by a golden tree. They entered, and a woman in a gold crown welcomed them. They saw a silver vat with gold hoops, full of red ale, and a golden cup and serving spoon. They saw a phantom which looked like a tall man on a throne (the Celtic god of light). The woman served them a meal, a 24-foot-long ox's rib and a boar's rib. The tall man recited a poem which told Conn how many years he would reign (35), and the names of the kings who would follow him.

Conn married Eithne Thaebfhota, and they had two sons named Connla and Art. The first son (Connla) fell in love with a fairy woman and went with her in her crystal boat to the land of faerie, leaving Art as the sole heir to the throne. After his mother's death, Art became the target of another fairy woman named Bé Chuille, who was banished to Ireland by the Tuatha De Danann. When she met his father Conn and learned that he was recently widowed, she agreed to marry him instead, on the condition that Art should leave Tara for a year. This caused a famine to occur during that year.

The men of Ireland thought that this famine could be ended by the sacrifice of the son of a sinless couple. Conn went in search of such a child and came to an island of apple trees. The queen of this island had a son, and Conn told her that he could save Ireland by bathing the boy in the water of Ireland. She agreed. The druids, however, demanded that the boy be sacrificed, but Conn, his son Art, and Fionn macCumhaill (the future son-in-law of Conn's grandson Cormac) protected him. By chance it happened that a woman driving a cow approached, so they sacrificed the cow instead. It had been carrying two bags, which they opened. One bag contained a bird with one leg; the other, a bird with twelve legs. The two birds then met in single combat, and the one-legged bird won. The woman said that the winning bird was the boy, and she herself was his mother, the queen of the apple-tree island. The twelve-legged bird represented the druids. She told Conn that the famine would end if he would banish his fairy wife, but he refused.

She was later banished from Tara after she and Conn's son Art played a series of games called *fidchell*, a Celtic board game similar to chess. However, *fidchell* had a mystical aspect to it. The gold and silver pieces moved themselves (as in *ouija* boards), and battles could ebb and flow as the game played on. Great events could be decided, depending on the outcome of the game.

83-m Art "the Solitary" Eanfhear

Conn reigned 35 years and was killed by Tipraiti Tireach, a descendant of Milesius' son Ir. Tipraiti sent fifty warriors dressed as women to kill him at the Hill of Tara. was succeeded by his son-in-law Conaire II (who had married Conn's daughter Saraid; they had three sons).

Conaire was murdered by Neimhidh (son of Sraibhgheann). Adding insult to injury, Neimhidh married Conaire's widow and hired a bodyguard named Darera, with whom Conaire's sons would have to wrestle if they wanted to visit her. These three sons (called *Cairbres* or "Strong Men" – Musc, Riada and Bascainn) took revenge against Neimhidh and his allies in the Battle of Cenn Abrad in Munster. The nine sons of King Oilioll Ólom of Munster (by Conn's daughter Maicniadh) joined them.

A dispute arose between Ailill Bare-ear's foster son Lughaid mac Con ("Son of a Greyhound") and his foster brother Éogan, son of Oilill Ólom, about a fairy musician they had found: each of them claimed the musician for himself. The king decided in favor of Éogan, but Lughaid claimed that it was an unfair judgment. Cairbre Musc wounded Lughaid mac Con in the thigh, so that he was forever lame, and exiled him from Ireland. Lughaid made an alliance with Benne Brit, son of the king of Britain, raised an army of foreigners and returned to Ireland. He defeated and killed Art in the Battle of Magh Mucruimhe in Connacht. Seven sons of Oilioll Ólom were also killed there.

According to legend, Art was given hospitality by a local blacksmith named Olc Acha, the night before the battle. It had been prophesied that a great dignity would come from Olc's line, so he gave Art his daughter Achtan to sleep with. Art's son Cormac was conceived that night. (However, Achtan might have been Art's official mistress, to whom he paid a dowry of cattle. His wife, and the mother of his other children, was Medb Leithderg nic Conan of Cualan.)

Art ruled from 186 to 195 AD.

84-m Cormac Ulfada (Longbeard)

One night while she was all in her sleep, Cormac's mother Achtan had a vision. As she lay asleep beside Art, she dreamed that her head was detached from her body, and that a huge tree grew out of her neck. This tree extended its branches all over Ireland, but the sea came upon it and laid it low. After this another tree grew out of the roots of the first, but a blast of wind came from the west and knocked it down. Achtan started awake, and she told the vision to Art.

"That dream will come true," said Art, explaining its meaning to her. "The head of every woman is her husband, and I shall be taken from thee [in the Battle of Magh Muchruimhe]. The tree that will grow out of thee is a son which thou wilt bear to me, who will be king of Ireland. The sea that will overwhelm him is a fish-bone which he will swallow and be choked on it. The tree that will grow out of the roots of the first is his son, who will also be king of Ireland. The blast of wind from the west that will overthrow him is a battle that will be fought between himself and the Fian. The Fian will slay him in that battle, but the Fian will not prosper after that."

This vision was fulfilled in Cormac and his son Cairbre Lithfeachair, since the demons choked Cormac as he was swallowing a fish-bone, and Cairbre Lithfeachair fell by the Fian at the Battle of Gabhra.

One day, when Cormac was in the house of Cleiteach, the druids were worshipping a golden calf in his presence. The druid leader Maelgenn asked Cormac why he was not worshipping the golden calf like the others. Though he lived 200 years before the arrival of Saint Patrick in Ireland, Cormac had converted to Christianity. "I will not worship an idol made by my own artisan," said Cormac. "It would be better to worship the person who made it, for he is nobler than the idol." Maelgenn the druid riled up the golden calf so that it jumped as if alive. "Dost thou see that, O Cormac?" asked Maelgenn. "I see it," said Cormac, "but I will worship only the God of heaven, of earth, and of hell." After this he began to eat a piece of a salmon. Then the demon sprites came and killed the king by choking him on a salmon-bone.

During his reign (227-266 AD), Cormac composed a textbook to preserve manners, morals and government. He was a famous author in laws, chronologies, and history. He established law, rule, and direction for each science and for contracts regarding the ownership of property. He assembled the chroniclers of Ireland at Teamhair and ordered them to collect all the chronicles into one book, the *Psalter of Teamhair*.

In 240, Cormac sailed across the sea and conquered Alba (Scotland). In 241, his family were massacred by Dunlang, son of the King of Leinster. In revenge, he ordered that thirty royal girls and a hundred maids each, along with twelve princes of the Leinster should be put to death.

In 265, Cormac's eye was put out by a lance thrown by Aenghus Gaibhuaibhtheach. He died, as was said before, in 266 AD.

85-m Cairbre Liffeachair

Cairbre Lithfeachair, son of Cormac, was called Cairbre Lithfeachair because it was near the Lithfe in Leinster that he was brought up. His mother was Eithne Ollamda daughter of Dunlaing. His father was Cormac "Longbeard." He married Aine ingen Finn, and then Hvarfiadh, Princess of Ireland.

He also married Hvarfiadh Princess of Ireland. He had a daughter named Sgeimsolas (Light of Beauty), and a man named Maolsheachlainn O'Faolain came to seek her as a wife. Fionn and the Fenians heard of this and demanded that he pay them tribute of twenty ingots of gold. He refused. They said either pay the gold, or they would accept the head of the princess. He assembled some friendly kings and nobles and explained that he could no longer bear this kind of tyranny. They went home to their respective provinces and decided to expel the Fenians from Ireland.

Cairbre sent fifty battalions to expel the Fenians. When the seven standing battalions of the Fenians assembled in one place, they sounded their musical horn, the Barr Buadh, their trumpets, and all their musical instruments, and then marched forth in properly arranged ranks and dense columns of brave heroes, strong and powerful in their might, to the mountain of Gabhra.

The hero-warrior Oscur kept a sharp look out for Cairbre; for he felt convinced that if he laid his eyes upon him the men of Eirinn would be unable to rescue him alive. The two sons of Cairbre, namely Conn and Art, met him, and he engaged in combat with both. At length Oscur severed off the head of Conn, and soon after cut off Art's head. He then proceeded to the battlefield in search of Cairbre: When Cuirbre heard his two sons had been slain by Oscur he hastened to engage him in combat. Cairbre cast his spear at him, which pierced him in the back, under the shoulder, and wounded his heart; he fell down on the spot, but exclaimed "Oh, no! it is the spear of Cairbre which pierces my body, by which it has been foretold I should fall!" And Cairbre was slain at the Battle of Gabhra by Simeon son of Cearb, one of the Fortuatha of Leinster, as was foretold by his grandmother.

He reigned 268-284 AD.

86-m Fiachadh Sreabthuine

Fiachaidh Sraibhthine was the son of Cairbre Lithfeachair. His mother was Aine (Erenn), daughter of Fionn mac Cumhaill. He married Aoife, daughter of Gaedal, King of Gall.

When Fiachaidh was king of Ireland, his son Muireadhach Tireach led his army in battle, for the king himself would not be allowed to fight. On a certain occasion Muireadhach went into Munster accompanied by his army and carried off hostages and spoils. Fiachaidh Sraibhtine happened to be at Dubhchumair with a lot of soldiers. His brother's three sons, that is the Collas,* had more soldiers nearby, helping Fiachaidh Sraibhthine.

When they heard of the success of the King's son in Munster, people generally said that he would inherit the throne of Ireland.

"What shall become of us if Muireadhach becomes king of Ireland after Fiachaidh?" asked the Collas of themselves. "What we had better do is to give battle to the old king, slay him and his army, and overcome his son when he comes against us."

Fiachaidh at that time had a druid with him who said: "Oh king, if thou overcomest the Collas and slay them, there will never be a king of thy offspring after thee in Ireland. If it be they who shall succeed and slay thee, there will never be a king of Ireland of their progeny."

"Well then," said the king, "I prefer to fall by the Collas, and the kingdom to pass to my descendants after me, than that I should slay the Collas, and that the sovereignty of Ireland should go to their descendants after them."

In 322 AD, the two armies got ready for battle and attacked each other from either side. Fiachaidh Sraibhthine was defeated and killed in that battle, as the druid had foretold of him.

* Cairioll, grandson of Cairbre Lithfeachair, was called Colla Uais. He was distinguished above the other Collas, since he held the sovereignty of Ireland, and the other Collas did not. He held the sovereignty of Ireland four years and was then banished with his brothers into Alba by Muireadhach Tireach, son of Fiachaidh Sraibhthine. The three Collas' mother was Aileach, daughter of Udhaire, king of Alba, the wife of Eochaidh Doimhlean.

87-m Muireadhach Tireach

Muireadhach married Muireann, daughter of King Fiachaidh of Cineal Eoghain; she became the mother of Eochaidh Muighmheadhon.

As to the Collas who were banished by Muireadhach into Scotland, they numbered three hundred. The king of Alba received them, and they remained there three years. Then they came back to Ireland—that is, Colla Meann, Colla da Chrioch and Colla Uais. Having been instructed by a Druid, they scolded Muireadhach with evil words that he might kill them, and that on him might be a curse, that would result in the sovereignty of Ireland going to their descendants. He did not oppose them, so they stayed with him, and were faithful to him.

They spent a long time after this in close friendship, and the Collas were leaders in battle for the king. Then the king told them that it was time for them to win territory for their descendants.

"In what territory dost thou wish us to make sword-land?"

"Rise out against the Ultonians," said he, "for ye have just cause of battle with them, since an attendant of the king of Ulster burned the beard or hair of Cormac son of Art with a candle in Magh Breagh."

Now, when Cormac had become king of Ireland, a strong force of the Ultonians (from Ulster) came against him and drove him into Connaught. After that they made peace with Cormac and got ready a feast for him in north Magh Breagh. It was there that an attendant of the king of Ulster burned Cormac's hair. And that deed was still unavenged.

King Muireadhach gave them a large army, and the Collas went into the province of Connaught. After this, the men of Connaught joined in their march with a force of seven battalions; and they reached Carn Achuidh Leithdheirg in Fearnmhagh. From that hill they fought seven battles against the Ultonians, that is, a battle each day for a week. Six of these battles were fought by the Connaughtmen, and the seventh by the Collas, in which Fearghus Fogha, king of Eamhain, was killed; and the Ultonians were defeated and pursued from Carn Achuidh Leithdheirg to Gleann Righe, and, after inflicting great slaughter on them, the Collas returned and attacked Emhain, which they plundered and burned, so that it has ever since remained without a king to inhabit it. On that occasion, the Collas wrested Modharnuigh, Ui Criomthainn, and Ui Mac Uais from the Ultonians. Colla Meann took possession of Modharnuigh, and Colla da Chrioch took Ui Criomhthainn, and Colla Uais took Ui Mac Uais. And Muireadhach Tireach fell by Caolbhaidh son of Cronn Badhraoi.

Muireadhach Tireach held the sovereignty of Ireland for thirty-three years, and was killed by Caolbhach son of Cronn Badhraoi. who reigned for one year.

88-m Eochaidh Moigmeodhin

Eochaidh Muighmheadhon, was the son of Muireadhach Tireach and Muireann ingen Fiachaidh. He held the sovereignty of Ireland seven years. He was called Eochaidh, because in his head and breast he resembled the king, and in his waist, he resembled a slave called Mionghadhach.

Eochaidh first married Mong Finn, daughter of Fiodhach, the mother of Brian, Fiachrach, Fergus and Ailill. His second wife was Cairenn (Carinna), daughter of King Scal Moen ("the Dumb") of Britain. She was mother of Niall Naoighiallach. A third wife was Eyvindr Princess of Mumhan, but they had no children together.

Eanna Cinnsealach, king of Leinster, won the battle of Cruachan Claonta over Eochaidh, and took the druid named Ceadnathach prisoner. Eanna came up and asked his men why they had spared the druid.

"Thou wouldst never conquer from this hill on which I am, if I were to live," said the druid. Upon hearing this Eanna ran him through with his spear. As the spear pierced his body, Eanna broke forth in laughter.

"Alas," said the druid, "that is a foul laugh."

Eanna Cinnsealach was powerful in his time, as may be seen from the poem composed by Dubhthach son of O Lughair, who was chief poet of Ireland when Patrick came to spread the Gospel in Ireland.

Mong Fionn was extremely jealous and tried to force her husband to drive Niall out and make Carinna work as a servant in their house. Niall was cast out temporarily, but he returned and had his true mother reinstated.

89-m Niall of the 9 Hostages (Niall Noigiallach)

During the time of his wife Mong's acting up, Eochaid set the boys to some tests of strength and character, telling them that whoever succeeded would inherit the throne.

For one of the tests, Eochaid sent the boys out hunting. When they came across an old hag guarding a well, she demanded a kiss from them in return for water. Grossed out, Aillil and Fergus went running for the hills. Only Brian and Niall remained. Brian gave the hag a quick peck on the cheek, whereas Niall went for it and kissed her passionately. The hag turned into a beautiful woman who was actually the Queen of Ireland. She rewarded Niall not only with the water but also promised him that he and twenty-six of his descendants would rule Ireland. This came true.

When Euchaid died, Mong Fionn arranged for her brother, Crimthann, to take the throne until her son Brian was old enough to become king, but Crimthann double-crossed her and took full control for himself. He was a very good king and reigned over Ireland for 20 years.

Finally Mong Fionn poisoned her brother in a desperate attempt to have Brian succeed to the throne. However, she drank from the same cup to avoid suspicion but died in vain. Carinna's son Niall became king, as was promised by the Queen during his father's test of courage.

Niall earned his nickname by taking members of his enemies' families and refusing to give them back until they admitted defeat. These enemies included four Ireland provinces (Connaught, Munster, Leinster, Ulster and Meath) plus Britain, the Picts, the Dalriads, the Saxons, and some Gauls from France. The Picts grew tired of Nialls' methods and attacked the small Irish colony of Dalriada, which was on the coast of Scotland. Niall retaliated by going to Scotia Minor* and taking more hostages. Next Niall and his allies marched south and took hostage a youth by the name of Succat and carried him off to Ireland. (This youth later escaped, but he returned later to become Saint Patrick.) Niall managed to take control over a northern part of Ireland where he created a dynasty that was to see his descendants reign as High Kings of Ireland for 600 years, ruling at the Hill of Tara.

Niall married Inne, daughter of Lughaidh. She was the mother of Fiachaidh. A second wife was Rioghnach ingen Meadaib, who bore him seven sons, namely, Laoghaire and Eanna, Maine, Eoghan (90-m), two Conalls, and Cairbre.

Niall was killed in 405 AD by the son of the king of Leinster by Eochaidh in Muir Nicht, which is what they called the English Channel

* The name of Scotland up to the time of Niall Naoighiallach was Alba. Before that time it was called Albania, derived from Albanactus, the third son of Brutus, since that was the share that his father left to him. Niall ordained that "Alba" should be changed to "Scotia Minor." Even when the Dal Riada permitted it to be called Scotia, they and their descendants kept the name Alba.

Naill of the Nine Hostages

In 428 AD Dathi (127th Monarch), son of Fiachrach (son of Mong Fionn) was killed by a flash of lightning. In 430 Pope Celestinus the First sent Palladius to Ireland to spread the Gospel. He landed in Leinster with 12 men. Three wooden churches were erected. He left a shrine with relics of St. Paul and St. Peter. He was not well respected in Ireland. He contracted a disease in Cruithnigh and died. In 434, Loarn, son of Eochaidh Muinreamhar, was born. He was Erc's younger brother.

90-m Eogan Find macNeill 400-465

Eogan MacNeill, born in 400 AD, was the son of Niall of the Nine Hostages and his wife Rignach ingen Meadaib. He was assumed to have been a close friend of Saint Patrick, who blessed him. A plaque at St. Patrick's Church in Iskaheen, Donegal, reads, "Eoghan Prince of Inis Eoghain, Son of Niall of the Nine Hostages. Died 465 of grief for his brother Conall [Gulban]. Baptised by Patrick and buried in Uisce Chaoin."

Among his sons were Muiredach mac Eogain, Fergus mac Eogain, and Angus mac Eogain.

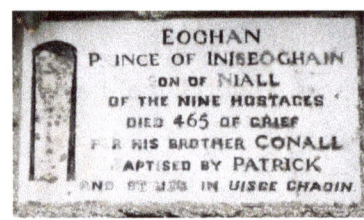

Saint Patrick

Saint Patrick was the patron saint of Ireland. He was born in Britain of a Roman-British family named Calpurn. His native town was Nemthor. His mother was named Cochnias. His father was Calphrann, son of Fotaide, son of Deisse, son of Cormac Mor, son of Lebriuth, son of Ota, son of Orric the Good, son of Moric, son of Leo, son of Maximus, son of Encretti, son of Philisti, son of Fereni, son of Brutus ("Otter of the Sea").

When Patrick was a teenager, he was captured by Irish pirates (or possibly Niall of the 9 Hostages) and sold as a slave. For the next six years, he worked as a herder in Ireland, turning to a deepening religious faith for comfort. Following the counsel of a voice he heard in a dream one night, he escaped and found passage on a ship to Britain, where he was eventually reunited with his family. After that, his father sent him to the Continent to train as a priest. In 431 Patrick was ordained bishop by Pope Celestine I, who ordered him to go to Ireland; he arrived in 432.

St Patrick was largely responsible for the expansion of Christianity in Ireland during the fifth century AD. He separated the Irish from the worship of idols and specters, who conquered and destroyed the idols which they had for worshipping. He expelled demons and evil spirits from among them, and brought them from the darkness of sin and vice to the light of faith and good works. He guided and conducted their souls from the gates of hell to the gates of heaven. It was he that baptized and blessed the men, women, sons and daughters of Ireland, with their territories and tribes. He used a three-leaf clover—the shamrock—to describe the Holy Trinity. He saw to it that many cells, monasteries, and churches were erected throughout Ireland: seven hundred churches in all. It was by him that bishops, priests, and persons of every dignity were ordained: seven hundred bishops and three thousand priests. He worked many miracles and wonders, including exorcising demons. At first, when Patrick met the bard Caílte and heard the ancient warrior's stories, he thought these pagan tales may corrupt his church believers. However his guardian angels, Aibelán and Solusbrethach, told him he should write down all the tales or poems that the heathen bard recited.

When the time of St. Patrick's death approached, he received the Body of Christ from the hands of the holy Bishop Tassach, and resigned his spirit to heaven at the age of one hundred twenty-two.

As a legendary figure St Patrick was said to have performed several miracles including destroying the gold icon of Crom Cruach and removing all the snakes on the isle. There were no snakes native to Ireland. The term "snakes" may be figurative and refer to pagan religious symbols rather than reptiles or amphibians. Remember the prophecy of Moses regarding the offspring of Goedel Glas?

Saint Patrick

Part 6
The Kings of Argyll

Argyll

Argyll (from *Airer Goedel*, "Coast of the Gaels") corresponds to the Irish Dal Riata. Its main clans are the Campbells and their close allies the MacIntyres; the Gregors and the MacLachlans. The name *Airer Goedel* replaced the name *Dal Riata* in the 9th century, when the Norsemen split Irish *Dál Riata* and the islands of Alban *Dál Riata* off from the mainland Alban *Dál Riata*. The Norsemen ruled these islands from the 9th to 12th centuries.

Dal Riata

Irish society developed from Eber, Heremon and Ir, the sons of Milesius. Starting about the 5th century AD, Irish seafarers began to expand across the North Channel, settling on the western coast of Scotland. This ancient kingdom was known as the Dál Riata (named after Conaire's son Eochaid Cairbre Riata). In Ireland, it included what is now County Antrim; in Scotland it included what is now Argyll. This was separated by mountains from the main part of Scotland, so the people continued to speak Gaelic rather than Pictish. There were four main families: those who descended from Gabran and Comgall (sons of Domangairt), and those who descended from Oengus and Loarn (sons of Eirc). The first king of Dál Riata was named Loarn mac Eirc. The last king (before the Vikings took over) was Diarmaid mac Sealbhaigh, who died in about 914 AD.

The Lords of the Isles

Generally the Lordship was thought to have begun around 1330 AD, but the history of this region actually stretches back another five hundred years to Gille Adomnan, who was married to the heiress of Godfrey McFergus (810-853), Lord of the Hebrides. The McFergus branch of the old royal family stayed in the Western Isles of Scotland to do battle with the invading Vikings who began attacking the Western Isles in 793 A. D.

The officially recognized Lords of the Isles include all the McDonalds, from Somerled (1115-1164) to Angus Og (d. 1330). At present, Prince Charles Windsor holds the title.

The Picts

The word "Pict" was a (slightly derogatory) term the Romans used in the 3rd century AD to describe the people who lived in northeastern Scotland, north of the Firth of Forth. In Latin, *pictus* meant "painted," a reference to the tattoos that those people wore. The Picts were descendants of the Caledonians, a Celtic tribal confederacy.

During the reign of the Pictish king Angus mac Fergusa (729-761), the Dal Riata was subject to Pictish rule. By the year 900 AD, the Picts had merged with the Dalriada to form the Kingdom of Alba.

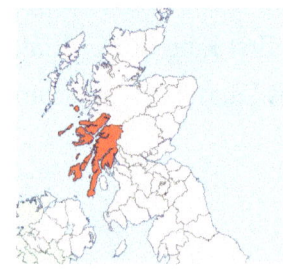

Map of Dal Riata   Argyll   The Isles

Table 6. Kings of Argyll + Kings of Scotland

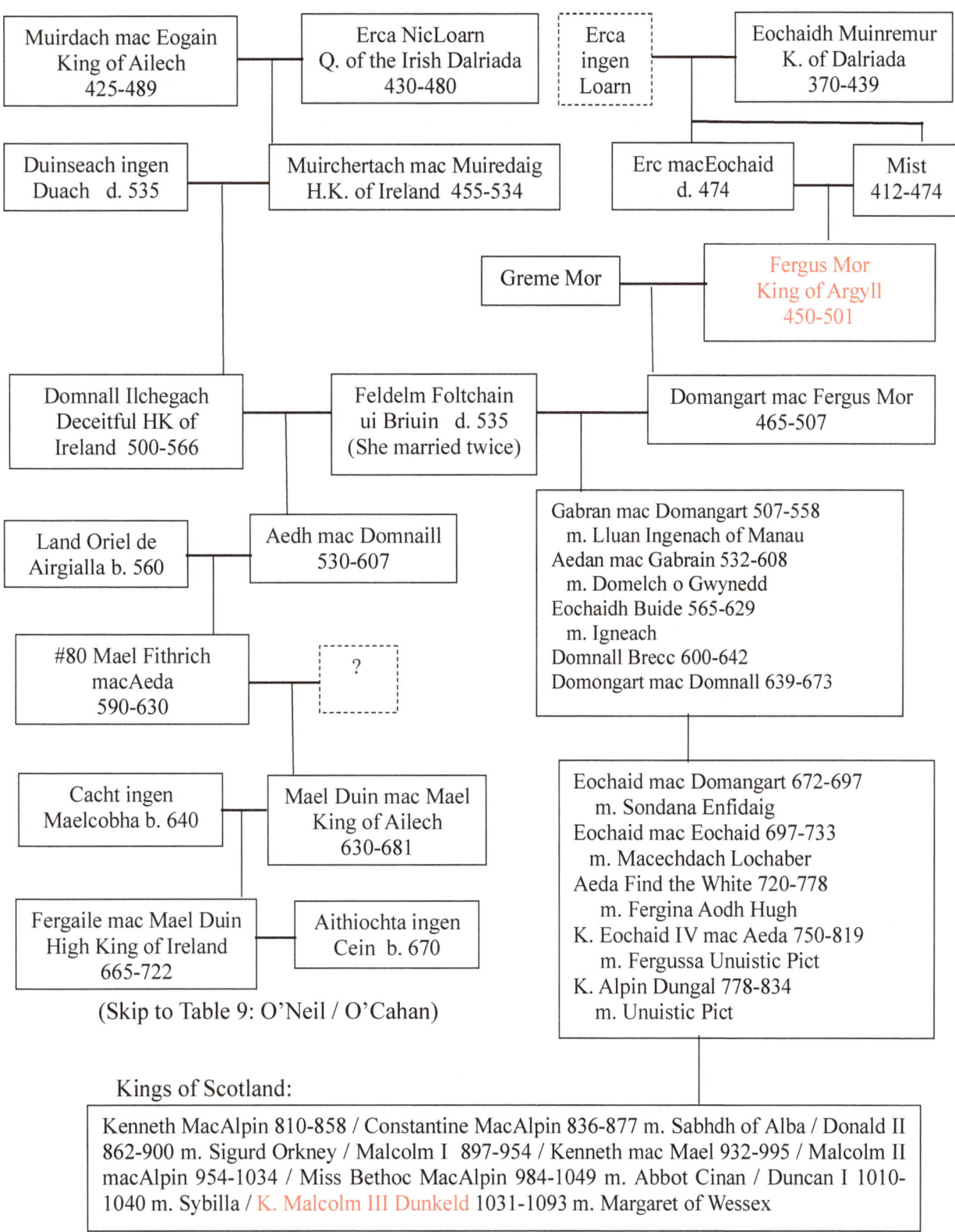

Kings of Scotland:
Kenneth MacAlpin 810-858 / Constantine MacAlpin 836-877 m. Sabhdh of Alba / Donald II 862-900 m. Sigurd Orkney / Malcolm I 897-954 / Kenneth mac Mael 932-995 / Malcolm II macAlpin 954-1034 / Miss Bethoc MacAlpin 984-1049 m. Abbot Cinan / Duncan I 1010-1040 m. Sybilla / K. Malcolm III Dunkeld 1031-1093 m. Margaret of Wessex

(Skip to Table 7: Huntingdon / Bruce / Stewart)

Earca nic Loarn

Earca nicLoarn was said to have been a daughter of Loarn, King of Dalraida (b. 355) in Alba (Scotland). Actually, there were probably two Earcas, as the name Loarn was fairly common at that time. Either that, or there was some mistake in recording their data, for the husband of one lived about one hundred years after the husband of the other.

The later husband, Muiredach mac Eogain (425-489) was the son of Eoghan Find MacNeill and Indorb (Marb) Find. He was also married to an Erca nicLoarn, known as the "Queen of the Irish Dalriada," who lived from about 430-480 AD. We will come back to this line after six generations, which will bring us to Fergail mac Mael Duin, High King of Ireland, ancestor of both the O'Neills and the O'Cahans.

For now, let us look into the lineage of the earlier husband, Eochaidh Muinremur.

91-m Eochaidh Muinremur

The earlier husband pf Earca, Eochaidh Muinremur (91-m 370-439) was father of Erc MacEochaid (92-m d. 474), who was father of Fergus Mor (93-m), as well as Loarn mac Erc and Oengus Mor mac Erc. Some say his wife Erca (b. 380 AD) was the daughter of Loarn mac Eirc. In fact, the mother of his son Erc was Carthn Casduff (b. 356).

Eaochaid was also said to have been drowned by his grandson, but the person who did it, Muirchertach, would have been his great-great-great-grandson – Muirchertach mac Earca, son of Muiredach mac Eogan, son of Eogan Find MacNeill, son of Niall mac Echach (89-m, Niall of the Nine Hostages). Such were the discrepancies in reporting dates in early Irish history.

92-m Erc

Erc MacEchach was the son of Eochaid Muinremar. Another son (Erc's brother) was named Olchu. By other accounts, Eochaid Muinremur was said to have married Fergusa (or Feidelmid).

Regardless of his own maternal ancestry, Erc mac Eochaid married a woman named Mist ingen Muiredaig (412-474) and had three sons: Fergus Mor, Loarn and Oengus (Angus, from *Aeneas*).

In the year 474, King Erc of Irish Dalriada died. The succession was in dispute, and their uncle was made King in accordance with the Celtic Law of Tanistry. The Caledonian crown came to rest once more on the head of an Irish king.

Olchu sent his nephews Loarn, Fergus, and Angus to become rulers in Caledonia. They landed in Kintyre in 503 AD and immediately set up separate governments. Loarn occupied the district still known by his name (Lorne). Fergus was allotted Islay and Kintyre, while Angus ruled Arran and Cowal. The deaths of Loarn and Angus soon left Fergus as sole monarch of the Caledonian Scots, until he died in 506 AD.

93-m Fergus Mor

Fergus Mor (430-501) is thought to have been the first king of Scotland. In 498 AD, Fergus went with his brothers Loarn and Angus to assist King Loarn in his fight against the Picts. Fergus and his men chased the Picts back to their own homes, to the point that they sued for peace. When old King Loarn died, Fergus Mor was elected king by a unanimous vote, being of royal blood through his mother Mist (of the line of Milesius).

Fergus wanted to be crowned on the Stone of Destiny (the stone upon which Jacob rested his head when he had his vision at Bethel (Gen. 28:10-22), possibly the same stone from which Moses drew water in the wilderness (Numbers 8:11). It had been brought to Ireland by Scota, who married Milesius of Spain. Fergus asked for the stone from his brother Muredoch in Ireland, who lent it to him. He never returned it, but finally it came to rest at Scone. In 1296 Edward I, King of England, carried it away to Westminster Abbey, where it still remains under the Coronation Chair (having survived several attempts to abduct it), though plans are under way to return the Stone to Perth.

From King Alpin to King Duncan I

Picking up from King Fergus Mor, we continue with Kings Dongard (94-m), Conran (95-m), Aidan (96-m), Eugene IV (97-m), Donald IV (98-m), another Dongard (99-m), Eugene V (100-m), Findan (101-m), Eugene VII (102-m, why not VI?), Etfinus (103-m), and Achaius (104-m). This brings us to King Alpin (105-m).

105-m King Alpin

Though his father was Eochaid IV, who had an Irish name, Alpin probably derived his name (Elphin) from his mother Urgusia, a Pictish princess (sister of Constantine mac Fergusa, King of the Picts).

In his wisdom, Alpin perceived the weakness of his neighbors beyond the Clyde. He desired to reign over richer people and more extensive domains. In 836 he set sail from Kintyre and landed on the coast of Kyle. Alpin resolved to remove the Picts and laid waste to the country between the Ayr and Doon rivers, before the people and their chiefs could defend themselves. Finally, Alpin defeated the Picts at Galloway, and the Pictish king was killed. However, a new king, possibly named Drest, was elected in his place.

Following the course of these rivers (Ayr and Doon) Alpin penetrated to the ridge which separates Kyle from Galloway, and here he was killed during a sharp struggle, from the obscure weapon of an enraged chief near the site of Laicht castle. It is said that Alpin's head was attached to a pole and carried around as a spectacle in Abernathy, the capital of the Picts.

Alpin had three sons: Domnall macAlpin, Kenneth macAlpin, and Grigair macAlpin.

King Alpin

106-m King Kenneth I

Born around 810 AD on the island of Iona, Kenneth was the son of Alpin, King of Dalriada. Kenneth became king in 843. He united the Scots and the Picts (it was more likely a conquest of Picts by Scots), thus founding the kingdom of Scotland. He reigned for 16 years as King of Alba, King of the Picts, and King of Dalriada.

During Kenneth's reign the Stone of Destiny was moved from Iona to Scone in order to avoid depravations by Vikings.

Kenneth MacAlpin died in 858 at Forteviot, a few miles southwest of Perth, and was buried on Iona. (On the crest of a small rise now called Halyhill, at the west end of the village, overhanging May water, stood Fortevieth, the ancient capital of Fortrenn. Angus MacFergus, King of the Picts, built a church, and his palace, here.)

His brother Donald became King after Kenneth died. No one knows the name of Kenneth's wife, though she may have been a Pictish princess. His children were Constantine, Aed of the White Flowers, Mael Muire ingen Cinaeda, and a daughter whose name is unknown, but she married the King of Strathclyde and had a son named Eochaid. Another daughter may have married Amlaib Conung, King of Dublin.

Ancient Scotland

107-m King Constantine I

There are suggestions that Constantine's mother may have been Pictish (possibly the daughter of Uurad (or Feradach son of Bargoit, the king of Picts from 839 to 842). Constantine became king when his uncle Domnall mac Alpin died in 862.

Like his uncle and father before him Constantine I spent much of his reign under attacks from the Vikings. In fact, Viking activity reached its peak during his reign. In 870, the Vikings Amlaib and Ivar attacked Dumbarton Rock and laid siege to the fortress for four months. In 871 the Vikings took Angles, Britons and Picts home as hostages. Constantine killed Amlaid either then or the next year. Ivar died in 873. Another great slaughter at the hands of the Danes occurred in 875 near Dollar or Atholl. Constantine built a new church at St. Andrews, but the Vikings caught up with him and killed him, either at Fife beach or at Newport-on-Tay, which matches the Prophecy of Berchan (a long historical poem given around the time of Saint Patrick, prophesying the life of 24 Scottish kings from Kennith macAlpin to Domnall Ban (d. 1097). He was killed by Vikings in 878. The plaque reads,

> "According to local tradition King Constantine I was killed in this cave, called the Nigra Specus or Black Cave, after a battle with the Dubhgall (dark foreigners or Danes) in 874. However accounts of Constantine's place and date of death do vary… The Danes were offered a safe refuge in his lands and the right to buy provisions to their hearts' content if they ceased from raids and faithfully observed the agreed terms of peace. So when they could not be pacified by a consideration of this kind or any other consideration involving peace, in the place called the Black Chasm (whether on a pre-arranged date or unexpectedly or accidentally is not known) the King joined battle with them and died with many of his men. It is not surprising since he rashly used certain of the Picts recently subdued to fight alongside him like a snake in his bosom. For they fled immediately battle was joined, so offering an opportunity for the rest to do the same; and so the King, deserted on the field of battle by a large part of his army, was surrounded and killed by the enemy. They themselves withdrew to their ships immediately after the victory. The Scots who had fled returned and after searching the plain found the dead body of the King and bore it to the island of Iona with great lamentation. He was buried there in his father's bosom with full honors."

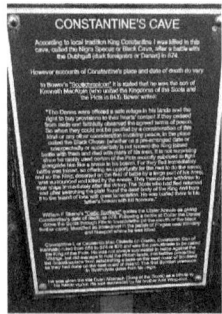

108-m King Donald II ("Dasachtach, the Madman")

Donald was the son of Constantine mac Kenneth. He became king after the death or ... of King Giric macDungail, probably around 889 AD.

The change from king of the Picts to king of Alba is important. He was the first king who was described by the Irish chroniclers as King of Alba. The Prophecy of Berchan places Donald's death at Donnattar, killed by Gaels rather than Norsemen, around 900.

His cousin Constantine II assumed the throne after Donald died, but another king may have reigned after his death "for half a day."

109-m King Malcolm I

Malcolm mac Domnaill was born in about 900 AD, the same year his father Donald died. He became king when his cousin Constantine II abdicated the throne and became a monk. Constantine's decision was not voluntary, according to the Prophecy of Berchan.

King Edmund I of England had chased Amlaib out of Northumbria in 945, at which time he allowed Malcolm to rule Strathclyde in return for his allegiance. Malcolm kept his agreement, which may have been honored by the new king, Eadred.

He died in 0954 in a shield wall in the Mearns, either at Dunottar (as in the Prophecy of Berchan) or at Fetteresso (as in the *Annals of Ulster*). He was buried either on the island of Iona or at Fetteresso Castle.

Malcolm's son Dub became King of Alba from 962-967. His son Kenneth became King of Alba from 971-995.

110-m King Kenneth II

Kenneth was the son of Malcolm I. There had been a feud between the descendants of King Indulf (r. 954-962), son of Constantine II, and Kenneth's family since 977, when Kenneth killed Indulf's son Amlaib. He married a "Lady of Leinster Ireland." Their son was Malcolm II.

Kenneth was killed in 995 by Finnguala, daughter of Cuncar, in revenge for killing her only son at Dunsinane. One day Kenneth and his companions went hunting in the woods, near Finnguala's house. She invited him to come for a visit, telling him she had news of a conspiracy. However, she had booby-trapped an out-of-the-way little cottage, attaching crossbows by strings to the head of a statue of a boy. Kenneth touched the statue and was shot through from all sides. She fled to St Cyrus, where she threw herself over a waterfall. Kenneth was buried in Iona, Scotland.

Some say Finnguala ("White Swan") was a mythical figure, a stream-goddess, daughter of Lir the sea-god, turned to a swan by her stepmother and cursed to roam Ireland for 900 years.

111-m King Malcolm II

Malcolm was born about 954, the son of King Kenneth II. The name of his mother is uncertain, but the Prophecy of Berchan says his mother was a "Lady of Leinster." However, some historians claim that his mother was Queen Boada, daughter of Constantine and granddaughter of some prince of Norway.

Malcolm was one of several kings in Scotland who reigned concurrently. Others were the king of Strathclyde, several Norse-Gael kings on the western coast, and the kings or mormaers of Moray. The earls of Bernicia and Northumbria in England still ruled most of the southeast.

In 1005 he killed Kenneth III, presume heir to the throne, in battle at Strathearn. Within a few days of his own coronation, Malcolm defeated a Norwegian army.

His wife may have been Gunnora, daughter of the second Duke of Normandy, but they had no sons. Malcolm tried to negotiate a series of dynastic marriages of his three daughters to men who might otherwise have been his rivals: Bethoc to Abbot Crinan, Thane of the Isles; Olith to Sigurd, Earl of Orkney; Donada to Finlay, Earl of Moray (a descendant of Loarn of Dalriada). Malcolm could not pass the kingdom down directly to his son, because he had only daughters.

During this period, the Scottish throne still passed in Picto-Gaelic fashion from brother to brother, uncle to nephew, or cousin to cousin. The way that Duncan I became king is noteworthy for being the beginning the transition to the Anglo-Norman system of primogeniture (meaning the oldest son inherited the throne).

Malcolm died in 1034.

King Malcolm II

112-m Bethoc ingen Mail Coluim (daughter of Malcolm)

Born in 984, Bethoc was the heir of King Malcolm II of Scotland. Around 1000 AD she married Abbot Crinan (of Dunkeld), Mormaer of Atholl.* Bethoc's married name became O'Neill. She was also known as Beatrix of Scotland. When married, she gained the title of Heiress of Scone, Lady of Atholl.

Bethoc's sister Donada married Findlaech mac Ruairi, and was the mother of MacBeth. Under the rules of tanistry, Malcolm II designated Duncan as his successor. Duncan became King of Alba in 1034. Macbeth murdered Crinan's elder son Duncan (see page 80).

Arms of Atholl

* The Mormaer of Atholl, was a medieval lordship (second only to the King of Scots, equivalent to English earls or Continental counts) in northern Perthshire. Atholl was an ancient Pictish kingdom. The first Earl of Atholl was Robert Stewart (1316-1390), who later became King Robert I of Scotland. In the Eighth Creation (1457) of the Earls of Atholl, five successive Earls were named John Stewart; a sixth John Stewart (1566-1603) assumed the title in the Ninth Creation.

113-m King Duncan I "the Gracious"

Duncan was born in 1013, the son of Abbot Crinan and Bethoc, daughter of King Malcolm II. In 1030, at the age of 17, he married Sybil Fitzsiward (1014-1040) (her Gaelic name was Suthen). Her father was Siward (or Sigurd) Bjornsson, Earl of Northumbria, a son of Biorn Ulsinsson, an Earl in Denmark.

Duncan may have been married earlier to a girl named Unfrida, a daughter of Gigurt, Earl of Northumbria, and also to Astrida, a daughter of King Sigfrid of Dublin.

Duncan became king in 1034 when his grandfather Malcolm II died. He ruled for six years until his own death in 1040. In the early part of Duncan's reign, his cousin Macbeth (Mac Bethad) served as his "dux," or duke, a rank between prince and marquess, which had the meaning of "war leader."

In 1040 Duncan led an army into Moray, which was MacBeth's domain, and was killed in action.

from a Frieze by William Hole, 1898

Macbeth (1005-1057) was the grandson of King Malcolm II, and his wife was the granddaughter of King Kenneth III. Under the ancient law of the Picts, he had as much claim to the throne of Scotland as did King Duncan I. He was commander for Duncan, whom he slew, making himself king. Scotland prospered during his reign, but he was later killed by the future King Malcolm III, the son of Duncan. If Macbeth had not been killed by Malcolm, Scotland would probably have remained a separate nation until this day, and might have conquered England.

The real Macbeth ruled 1040 to 1057 and had little in common with the unsavory character portrayed in Shakespeare's play (ca. 1606). He slew his rivals on the battlefield, not in the bed chamber. He did in fact die in battle – at Lumphanan - not when Birnam Wood moved to Dunsinane as Shakespeare wrote. He ruled wisely and generously, finding time to make a pilgrimage to Rome, where he scattered money among the poor like sowing seeds on a field.

Table 7. HUNTINGDON / BRUCE / STEWART

- K. Malcolm III 1031-1093 — Margaret of Wessex 1045-1093
  - K. David I ~1085-1153 — Matilda of Huntingdon 1074-1131
    - Prince Henry 3rd Earl of Huntingdon ~1114-1152 — Ada Warenne ~1120-1178
      - Marjory of Huntingdon ~1152-1213 — Gilchrist de Angus 1142-1204
        - Bethoc Angus ~1184-1252 — Walter Stewart III 1180-1246
          - Alexander Stewart IV ~1214-1283 + Jean Macrory
            - James Stewart V ~1260-1309 + Egidia Burgh
              - Walter Stewart VI ~1293-1326 — Marjorie Bruce 1294-1317
          - Margaret Stewart 1206-1255 — Niall 2nd of Carrick 1202-1256
            - Marjory of Carrick ~1252-1292 — Robert de Brus ~1243-1304
              - K. Robert Bruce 1274-1329 — Isabella de Mar Countess of Carrick ~1278-1302
                - Marjorie Bruce 1294-1317
      - David E. Huntingdon ~1144-1219 — Mathilda Chester 1171-1233
        - Isabelle of Huntingdon ~1199-1252 — Robert de Brus ~1144-1219
          - Robert de Brus 1210-1295 — Isabel de Clare 1226-1264
            - Robert de Brus ~1243-1304

From Malcolm III to Marjorie Bruce

114-m King Malcolm III

Margaret (1045-1093) was born in Hungary, daughter of the English Prince Edward Aetheling (the Exile) and his wife Agatha von Bayern. Prince Edward was considered a possible successor to Edward the Confessor, so they were recalled to England in 1057, but the prince died almost immediately upon landing. Twelve-year-old Margaret continued living at the royal court. The King himself died in 1066 and was succeeded by Harold Godwinson. After the Battle of Hastings in 1066 (where Harold was killed), Margaret's brother Edgar was proclaimed king, but the Normans had other plans, removing him temporarily to Normandy. Returning to England, the widowed Agatha planned to return to the continent in 1068, but a shipwreck carried them to Scotland. King Malcolm III (a widower with two sons, Donald and Duncan) found her irresistible (he had had his eyes on her as early as 1059, though she was not betrothed to him at that time), and though she had wanted to enter a nunnery, by the end of 1070, she was married. Their children included three kings of Scotland – Edgar, Alexander I, and David I, and one queen – Edith (renamed Matilda).

Pope Innocent IV sainted Margaret in 1250. She made a number of reforms to the Church in Scotland, such as changing the manner of observing Lent (beginning on Ash Wednesday instead of the following Monday), and observing the Sabbath on Sunday instead of Saturday. She washed the feet of the poor every day before she ate, and she used a cave as a place of devotion and prayer. She established a ferry across the Firth of Forth (near Edinburgh) for pilgrims who were traveling to St. Andrews. She spent much of her time praying, reading, and embroidering. The illiterate Malcolm had her books decorated in gold and silver. Her feast day is Nov. 16.

Margaret died of grief in 1093, three days after her Malcolm and their oldest son Edward were killed in the Battle of Alnwick, Northumberland.

Margaret's Lineage:
   Woden (Odin) of Asgard
   Baldaeg of the Aesir
   Brand of Scandinavia
   + 15 Generations
   Eoppa of Wessx
   Eaba of Wessex
   Ealhmund of Kent
   Egbert III
   Ethelwulf

Margaret's Lineage, Continued
   Alfred "the Great"
   Edward I "the Elder"
   Edmund I
   Edgar "the Peaceful"
   Ethelred II "the Unready"
   Edmund II "Ironside"
   Edward "the Outlaw"
   (Saint) Margaret of Wessex

Malcolm Welcomes Margaret

115-m King David I of Scotland

Malcolm III and Margaret of Wessex had eight children, including Edgar (b. 1074), Alexander (b. 1078), Edith (b. 1080) and David (b. 1084).

David spent most of his childhood in Scotland, but he was exiled along with two of his brothers to England in 1093 when his father and eldest brother were killed. There he became a ward of Henry I, who was the fourth son of William the Conqueror. When William died, two of his older sons vied for the English crown, but when William Junior ("Rufus") died in a hunting accident, Henry seized the crown and married David's sister Edith, who then became Queen of England (and changed her name to Matilda). Meanwhile David's brothers Edgar and Alexander each assumed the throne in Scotland in due order.

In 1113, King Henry gave David the hand of Matilda (Maud), the great-niece of William the Conqueror, in marriage. Maud was the daughter of Waltheof, Earl of Huntingdon (the only English aristocrat to be executed during the reign of William I), and his French wife Judith of Lens. She was also a descendant of Alfred the Great and Charles the Bald. They had 4 sons, 2 daughters. One son was named Henry after David's dear patron, the King.

David was not well-liked in Scotland, for he had spent too much time in England and Normandy. So when David's brother Alexander died in 1124, the Scottish aristocracy could either accept David as king or face war with both David and Henry I of England. Alexander's son chose to go to war, but David defeated him.

As king, David was instrumental in securing innovations in the Scottish Church. He increased the number of bishops from three or four to nine, and restored the bishopric of Glasgow. He appointed a French chaplain named John to the bishopric and carried out an inquest. There were some disputes between Scotland and the Archbishop of York, but Pope Honorius II wrote to John, ordering him to submit to York.

David died in 1153. He is recognized as a saint by the Roman Catholic Church, having a feast day on May 24, though he was never formally canonized.

The Seal of David   David I and Malcolm IV

116-m Prince Henry of Huntingdon

Ada de Warrenne, daughter of William, 2nd Earl of Surrey, was born in 1120. She married Prince Henry in 1139. As part of her dowry, the new Countess Ada was given Haddington, the first Royal burgh in Scotland, which had belonged to her father-in-law. Henry died in 1152, one year before his father King David I. Henry and Ada's son Malcolm (IV) became king at eleven years of age (Donnchad, Mormaer of Fife, served as regent until Malcolm grew up).

Malcolm faced a rebellion led by Malcolm mac Heth (macBeth), who was aided by Somerled, Lord of the Isles. They sacked Glasgow and attempted to take Renfrew, but Somerled (see below) was killed.

In 1165 the young King Malcolm died (he was 24), but he was unmarried and had no son. Ada's younger son William the Lion then became king of Scotland at age 23.

Ada devoted her time to good works, improving the Church at Haddington. She gave lands south and west of the River Tyne to found a convent of Cistercian Nuns (White Nuns). Religious houses of Blackfriars and Greyfriars were established after 1219.

Her other children were Ada, Margaret, David, 8th Earl of Huntingdon (who married Matilda of Chester; their daughter Isobel was the great-grandmother of Robert the Bruce), Matilda (Maud), who died unmarried, and Marjorie, who married Gille Crist, another ancestor of Robert the Bruce (see Table 7).

Ada died in 1178.

King Malcolm & King William

117-m Earl David of Huntingdon

Matilda, Countess of Huntingdon, was sometimes known as Maud de Kevelioc. Born in 1171, she was the eldest daughter of Hugh de Kevelioc, 5th Earl of Chester. Her mother was Bertrade de Montfort, a cousin of King Henry II of England. Her father died in 1181. Though his estates had Been confiscated, they were returned to him, and Matilda, along with her brother Ranulf, inherited them.

In 1190 Matilda married David (1152-1219), 8th Earl of Huntingdon, who was almost 20 years older than her. David and Matilda had seven children: Margaret (1194-1228), Robert, Ada, Matilda, John, Henry, and Isobel (1199-1251), mother of Robert de Brus.

David of Huntingdon

118-m Isobel of Huntingdon

Isobel was born in 1199, the younger daughter of Earl David and Matilda of Chester. She married Robert Bruce V, Lord of Annandale, about 1219. Isobel brought with her to the marriage the manors of Writtle and Hatfield Broadoak in Essex, England. Robert died in 1232, and she did not remarry, though together they had three children: Robert de Brus, Bernard de Brus, and Beatrice de Bruce.

119-m Robert le Brus IV

Lady Isabel de Clare of Gloucester and Hertford, born in 1226, was the youngest daughter of Isabel Marshal, the 4th Countess of Pembroke. Her father, Gilbert de Clare, Earl of Hertford and Gloucester, was one of the English noblemen who signed the Magna Carta.

In 1240, at the age of thirteen, Isabel married Robert de Brus (1210-1295). However, she died in 1264 (it may have been 1271, for in that year she was recorded as having received a gift of deer from King Henry I in Essex, England).

Robert served as regent during the childhood of Alexander III (grandson of William the Lion). All three of Alexander's children died, then Alexander himself fell off his horse and died in 1286. He was found lying alone on the beach. His granddaughter Margaret, Maid of Norway, was named as his successor, but she perished near the Orkney islands four years later. This Margaret was the last living descendant of William the Conqueror.* With no surviving male heirs of Alexander, David of Huntingdon's descendants were then the most likely candidates for the throne. Robert de Brus pleaded tanistry, supposing he was next of kin, though John Balliol had a better claim, as his ancestor was older. King Edward I also had his fingers in this pie: he appointed twenty-four auditors, whom he combined with forty auditors each for Bruce and Balliol; this court decided upon the latter. When Balliol died in 1314, Isabel's grandson Robert the Bruce became King of Scotland.

Isabel de Clare

* William the Conqueror → Henry I → Empress Matilda → Henry II → King John → Henry III → Margaret Plantagenet m. Alexander III of Scotland → Margaret, Heiress of Scotland m. Eric III of Norway → Margaret, Maid of Norway (1283-1290). As an infant, Margaret was betrothed to the future Edward II of England, which might have led to a United Kingdom, but she was lost at sea en route to England.

120-m Robert de Brus V (1243-1304)

In 1270, Robert and his father joined the retinue of Edmund of Lancaster and Edward, Duke of Gascony (the future King Edward I) on a crusade to the Holy Land (Lord Edward's Crusade, or the Ninth Crusade). They fought for nearly two years before returning to Scotland.

When his fellow crusader Adam de Kilconquhar died at Acre (north of Jerusalem) in 1271, the 27-year-old Robert was obliged to travel to tell the sad news to Adam's widow Marjorie of Carrick (daughter of Margaret Stewart, granddaughter of Walter Stewart, 3rd High Steward of Scotland). Finding the countess out riding, what happened next took everyone by surprise: Marjorie was so taken with the handsome young messenger that she held him captive until he agreed to marry her:

"She met a distinguished and very handsome young knight by the name of Robert de Brus. When greetings and kisses had been given on each side, as was the custom of courtiers, she begged him to stay for hunting and walking about. When he resisted, she by force, with her own hand, pulled back his reins and brought the knight, unwillingly to her castle of Turnberry. While staying there, for the fifteen days or more, he secretly married the Countess. They had in no way obtained the royal consent for the marriage, and because of this it was the common talk of the realm that she had all but carried off this young man into marriage by force."

Alexander III, King of Scots, soon forgave them. The marriage meant that Robert VI became *jure uxoris* (by right of his wife) Earl of Carrick. The earldom was valued at £168 and effectively doubled the Brus's income. Scotland in the thirteenth century had thirteen earls, and in an age before dukedoms were common either in Scotland or in England, Robert VI had overnight become a richer than his father Robert V, Lord of Annandale, but his father's formidable reputation still allowed him to rule over the family.

Robert VI and Marjorie had at least seven children. On July 11, 1274, their first son and heir was born. They named him Robert (a family tradition, it seems). This Robert Bruce would later go on to wear the Scottish crown.

Marjorie Marries Robert de Brus

121-m King Robert "the" Bruce I

Robert the Bruce was born in 1274. At the age of twelve, Robert first stepped out of the shadows of history when he, and a few others, placed his John Hancock as witness to a charter of Alexander MacDonald of Islay, who granted patronage to the Cistercian abbey of Paisley.

As a young noble child, he studied the arts of horsemanship, swordsmanship, the joust, hunting and perhaps aspects of courtly behavior, including dress, protocol, speech, table etiquette, music and dance, some of which he may have learned before the age of ten. Robert's later performance in war certainly proves his skills in tactics and single combat.

Isobel de Mar was the daughter of Domhnall I, Earl of Mar, and Elena, daughter of Llywelyn the Great. Isobel's father used her to strengthen ties with the Bruce family. At the time, Robert's grandfather Robert de Brus (see above) was vying for the throne. The House of Bruce was also politically motivated to marry Robert to Isobel. The territory ruled by the Earl of Mar was just south of Garioch, a land divided between four families, including the Bruces. Others were John Balliol and John Hastings. The fourth was Nichlas Biggar, who held a legal claim to Garioch. The House of Bruce sought a marriage with Clan Mar to strengthen their claim to Garioch.

Isobel gave birth to Marjorie in about 1296, but she died shortly thereafter, at the age of nineteen. Six years after the death of Isobel, Robert married Elizabeth de Burgh, a noblewoman born in Ulster, Ireland. She was the daughter of the Earl of Ulster, a close friend of King Edward I of England.

Robert was crowned King of Scots in 1306. Little by little he gained control of much of Scotland, then in 1314, at the Battle of Bannockburn, he defeated the much larger army of Edward II, making Scotland an independent kingdom. Pope John XXII recognized Robert as king, and when Edward II was deposed, his son Edward III renounced all claims of sovereignty over Scotland.

Robert I died in 1329. Although he failed to fulfill his vow to undertake a crusade, he appointed his nephew Thomas Randolph, Earl of Moray, as regent until his son David (then five) could reach adulthood. Robert was buried at Dunfermline Abbey. His only child by Isobel de Mar was Marjorie Bruce, who married Walter Stewart, the 6th High Steward of Scotland.

Robert and Isobel

122-m Marjorie Bruce (1296-1316)

When her father Robert the Bruce murdered his chief rival John Comyn in 1306, the English King Edward marched north to depose him. Recently crowned King, Robert eluded his English pursuers and sent his family to Kildrummy Castle to live with his brother Neil. When Edward II, Prince of Wales, laid siege to the castle, they bribed a blacksmith with all the gold he could carry to set fire to the grain store, and captured the castle. Neil was drawn and quartered, but the Earl of Atholl escaped with Robert's second wife (Elizabeth), his sisters Mary and Christina, and Marjorie. However, they were betrayed and handed over to the English, who executed Atholl. Elizabeth and Marjorie (then twelve years old) were held hostage for nearly a decade.

According to the *Flowers of History*, a cage was built for Isabella MacDuff, who oversaw Robert the Bruce's coronation. King Edward ordered:

> *Because she has not struck with the sword, she shall not die by the sword; but, on account of the unlawful coronation which she performed, let her be closely confined in an abode of stone and iron, made in the shape of a crown, and let her be hung up out of doors in the open air at Berwick, that both in her life and after her death she may be a spectacle and eternal reproach to travelers.*

Marjorie's aunt Mary (Robert's sister) was held in a similar cage outside Roxburgh Castle. A cage was built for Marjorie outside the Tower of London, but Marjorie was sent instead to the Gilbertine convent in Watton, where she lived for seven years. She was released as part of the ransom for Humphrey de Bohun, Earl of Hereford, who was captured at the Battle of Bannockburn.

Walter Stewart, 6th High Steward of Scotland, was sent to the border between England and Scotland to escort Marjorie and her stepmother Elizabeth de Burgh, once they were released.

Marjorie married Walter Stewart, but she died after falling off her horse near Paisley. Her son Robert was born by Caesarian section. He later became King Robert II. His daughter Margaret (123-m, Marjorie's granddaughter) married John McDonald (#98), Lord of the Isles.

Marjorie Bruce

Table 8. THE DONALDS

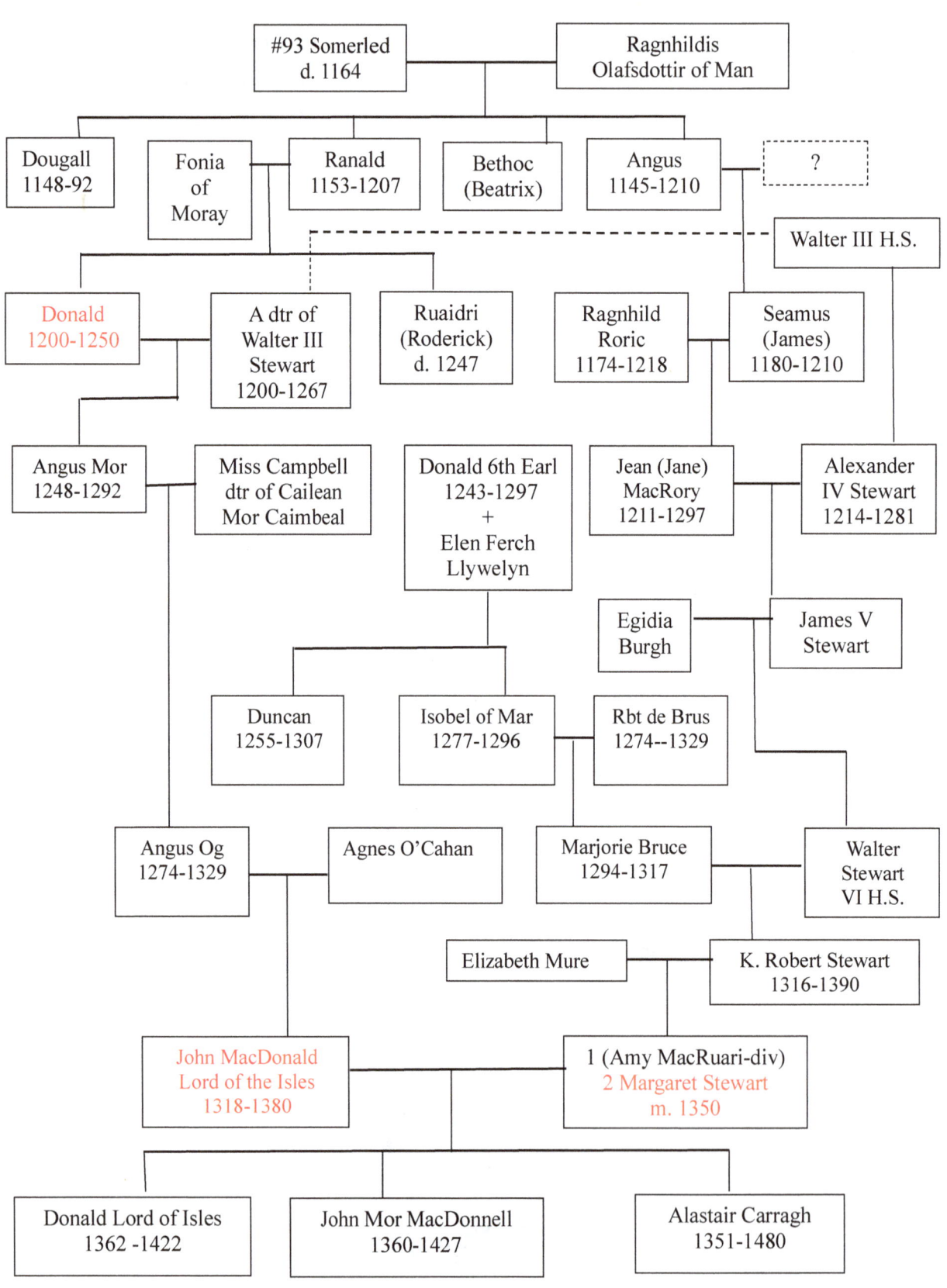

From Somerled to John Mor Tanister

#93 Somerled MacGillebride

Somerled (ca. 1115-1164) is regarded as the founder of the McDonald Clan. He was born either in Argyll (part of Scotland) or in Ireland. His mother was likely of Norwegian heritage, as the Isles at that time were controlled by Norway, but he was the first Lord of the Isles who was not strictly Norwegian. His wife was Ragnhild (or Sabina), daughter of Olaf Bitling, King of Man. She was also the great-granddaughter of Harald Hardraada of Norway (defeated by Harold Godwinson at Stamford Bridge).

His father Gillebride was Lord of Argyll. (Gillebride means "Servant of St. Bridgit," who was one of Ireland's patron saints. The Hebrides were once known as "Bride's Isles.") Somerled's name means "Summer Soldier" in Norse, and is pronounced "Sorley" in English.

After he removed the Scandinavians from Argyll, Somerled became a Thane. When his father-in-law died, he sailed with eighty ships and claimed the kingdom of the Isle of Man, eventually running the unpopular son of Olaf (by now his brother-in-law) out of power. Somerled also ruled the Isles, which included the Hebrides and the west coast of Scotland.

In 1157, Somerled helped a neighboring clan rebel against Malcolm IV. Somerled was granted the Norwegian title of King of the Sudreys, and eleven years of peace ensued between Somerled and Malcolm IV.

In 1164, Somerled took 15,000 men in 184 ships up the River Clyde to Renfrew. He died either in battle or before the Battle of Renfrew. The Scottish commander was (possibly) Walter FitzAlan, 1st High Steward of Scotland.

Two of his sons, Ranald and Angus, are important ancestors of the McDonalds. Angus was the grandfather of Jean MacRory, who married Alexander Stewart, 4th High Steward of Scotland. Ranald's son was the original Donald, the father of all the McDonalds. (This Donald also married an unnamed daughter of Walter Stewart, 3rd High Steward of Scotland, in other words, Alexander's sister, or possibly his half-sister.)

Somerled

#94 Ranald MacSomahairle

Ranald was born in 1153, son of Somerled and Ragnhild. Ranald became Lord of Oergeal and Cantyre, founder of Cistercian Monastery, Benefactor of Abbey of Paisley. Ranald's wife was named Fonia, possibly a latinized version of Fionnghuala, daughter of Ranulf Moray (of the Dunkeld dynasty) and Bethoc MacFergus of Galloway. Their son Donald was the original Donald, father of all the McDonalds. Another son, Ruadri, seems to have been the elder.

Ragnall styled himself King of the Isles, Lord of Argyll and Kintyre, and Lord of the Isles (*rex insularum*). His claim to the title of king was derived through his mother Ragnhildr, a member of the Crovan dynasty (who ruled the isles north of the Isle of Man by the strength of their galleys, a type of ship). Her father Olaf's father was named Godred Crovan.

The heraldic emblem of the MacDonalds in western Scotland features the galley, symbol of the island home. Some ancient arms have a lion rampant (the Lion of Judah), oars in action, and a red severed hand (symbol of Donald, who cut off his hand that he might win the island promised by the Chief of his galley – see below.) The mailed hand holding the Cross is emblematic of St. Patrick's appreciation of MacDonnell assistance. The fish is another symbol, which also comes from a story of Somerled. The people wished him to be their ruler and deliver them from the Norwegians. He said, "Islesmen, there is a newly run salmon in the black pool yonder. If I catch him, I will go with you." He caught the salmon, and so it figures today in the Coat of Arms.

Ranald probably founded Iona Abbey. Friars from Iona had relocated to Kells during the Viking onslaught. Somerled had tried to reinstate the abbey at Iona but encountered resistance from the locals. Ranald, however, was more successful, establishing a Benedictine monastery on Iona. A nunnery was also established at about the same time. Ranald died about 1207, or possibly he retired and went to live in Paisley Abbey.

Ranald's Seal (Reverse) Ranald's Seal (Obverse)

#95 Domhnall MacRaghnaill (The Original Donald)

Domhnall was born in Scotland in 1200 AD, the son of Ranald and Fonia of Moray. His vast impact on culture remains today.

Once when invading the Isles, the commander of the galley he was on swore that the warrior whose hand first touched the land before them should own that land forever. Hearing that, Donald sprang to the prow of the galley, cut off his hand with his own dagger, and cast the bleeding hand far onto the shore. That is the reason that the coat of arms carries a red hand (though some claim that it was the red hand of Zarah that inspired this emblem).

Before he died, Donald made a pilgrimage to Rome in penance for his sins, which were not imaginary. Once, King Alexander II of Scotland sent a messenger demanding Donald's allegiance to the Scottish Crown, but Donald sent the severed head of the messenger back to the king. Donald received absolution from the Pope after having declared his willingness to suffer any torment for his sins, even to the point of being boiled in a cauldron of lead (which luckily he did not have to endure). Returning to Scotland, Donald built a monastery to the honor of the Blessed Virgin.

It is important to note that Donald married a daughter of Walter Stewart, the 3rd High Steward of Scotland. Sadly, no one has been able to learn her name. [Elizabeth? Beatrix?] Was she that unimportant? Regardless, Donald left to his son Angus Mor a lordship of respectable size centered on Islay (the Isles). He gave his younger son Alasdair Mor some leftover lands, comprising every house from Mull to Kintyre. Donald died in 1293.

To the Unnamed Daughter of Walter Stewart

Here in the shade, time slips through my fingers
Like ripples o'er the Cora Linn falls.
Has it been long since I first left Renfrew?
Or was it only yesterday that I chased the geese
In the cloisters of Paisley Abbey?

My father was famous—the Third High Steward,
But as for my mother—I don't quite remember.
Perhaps she was Beatrix, Countess of Angus.
My brother was killed in the Crusade;
How dreadful, to die by the sword in Egypt.
My son, too, was famous—the first McDonald,
But who was I? Why can't I recall?

Here in the shade, I sit on the Abyss
Of the bright, glittering Universe,
The stars seem to ebb and flow like the tide
Upon the sand; I dip my toes in a pool.

But who was I? Why can't I recall?

#96 Angus Mor (the Great) MacDonald, Lord of the Isles

Angus Mor was born in Scotland in 1248, the son of the original Donald and *Sin Nomine* Stewart. During this time (around 1263), the kings of Norway were very aggressive towards Scotland. Angus Mor grudgingly supported the Norwegians in harassing King Alexander III of Scotland. However they failed to overcome the Scottish king, and the men of the Isles had to submit to Scotland. Angus was forced to hand over his son Alasdair Og as a hostage. Adding insult to injury, he was required to attend a council at Scone in which Margaret, Maid of Norway, was recognized as the rightful heir to the Scottish throne.

Angus married a daughter of Cailean Mor Caimbeal (Colin Campbell) and his wife *Sin Nomine* nic Duncan mac Duibhne of Lochow. She was the mother of Angus Og, Alasdair Og (named after Alexander III of Scotland), Iain Sprangach and a daughter named Mora who married a man named Ferquhar of the Clan Mhic an Toisigh (MacKintosh):

> *"Ferquhard's intercourse with the fair Mora of Isla was at first of an unauthorised character, and that, this being discovered, the lover fled to avoid the wrath of her powerful father. He took refuge in Ireland, but before he had been there long he was recalled, and on his return made Mora his wife."*

In February of 1293, three new sheriffs of western Scotland were created: the Sheriff of Sky, with territories associated with the Crovan dynasty, the Sheriff of Lorn, with territories spanning much of Argyll, and the Sheriff of Kintyre (this position was held by James Stewart, 5th High Steward).

When Angus Mor died in 1293 on the island of Islay, his son Alasdair Og succeeded him as Lord of the Isles.

Alexander III of Scotland

Alasdair Og MacDonald

#97 Angus Og MacDonald
Lord of the Isles

Angus Og was born in Scotland in 1274, the son of Angus Mor and Miss Campbell his wife. In 1299, he married Agnes O'Cahan, who gave birth to "Good" John MacDonald (see below).

Angus had another son, also named John (or Iain, b. 1300) Fraoch, by a daughter of Dougall MacHenry (macEanruig), who was born in Glencoe, Scotland. Lefthanded marriages, or trial marriages (also known as *handfast* marriages), were common in those days. Even with children, the wife was sometimes sent back to her own people if things didn't work out. This John Froach became the progenitor of the MacDonalds of Glencoe. (His descendants lived in caves long after their cousins of Glengarry were living in houses.)

In 1308, Angus succeeded his brother as chief of the Clan and Admiral of the Western Isles. In the struggles against England, Angus always chose the side of Robert the Bruce, and in the decisive battle (the Battle of Bannockburn in 1314) Bruce's words, "My hope is constant in thee," became the motto of the Ranald branch of Clan Donald. It remains so even to this day.

In 1330, Angus Og died in his castle in Islay and was laid to rest in the tomb of his ancestors on the Isle of Iona, where his gravestone is still to be seen.

Agnes O'Cahan was a daughter of Guy O'Cahan. She was born in Limvady, Ulster, Ireland. She was first married to Prince Muinhear Ceannfada O'Neill, with whom she had a son named Brian Balloch O'Neill (d. 1425).

Her lineage is as follows: Conchobhar ("Lover of Hounds"), Prince of Limavady; Gruagan (Irish, *hairy man*) Buchanan; Dungan; Cathain (Irish, *battle*); Cathusach; Dermod; Conn Cionntach – he had a brother named Annselan, ancestor of O'Bocainain (Irish, *fairies*) the first family who settled in Scotland; Giollachriosd; Iomhar; Ranall; Eachmarcach; Donall; Rory; Magnus Catha an Duin, Prince of Limavady, killed by the English in the Battle of Down (1260); Guy; Agnes (Cumach).

Aka Lady Margaret O'Cathan, Agnes brought a large force of Irish soldiers to her husband as a dowry. These are the O'Millans from Roe Water; the Roses; the Fearns, and the Beatons.

On a Chancery Roll dated 1338, Agnes, the mother of John of the Isles, is granted safe conduct, or permission to cross the channel to and from Ireland as often as she wishes to do so.

Angus Og of Islay

O'Cahan

#98 "Good" John MacDonald of Islay

John MacDonald was born in Scotland in 1318. His epithet "Good" was due more to his gifts to the Church, than any saintly quality of character. His first marriage was to his distant cousin Annie MacRuari, but he received special permission from the Pope to divorce Annie for no apparent reason (well, the reason was political – he needed to establish ties with the Scottish royal family). Then John married Margaret Stewart (b. 1342), daughter of King Robert II and Elizabeth Mure. Margaret was the granddaughter of Marjory Bruce, who married Walter Stewart, 6th High Steward of Scotland.

In 1356 John was taken prisoner fighting under the French banner at Poitiers. He was held captive by the English until December 1357 when he was allowed to return home. In 1360 he was appointed Constable of Edinburgh Castle, and in 1364 he held the high office of Seneschal of the King's Household.

After Robert II became king in 1371, the Crown maintained friendly relations with the Lord of the Isles, thanks to their close connection by marriage. John based his lordship around Finlaggan on Islay where his parliament met on an island in the middle of a loch. The parliament, or council, was made up of 16 men representing the different classes of society at that time - four lords, four sub-lords, four squires and four freemen. Appeals of decisions made by judges in the different territories of the lordship could also be made to this body. According to the *Annals of the Four Masters*, John died at Ardtornish Castle in 1387 and was buried in Iona.

The plaque below reads, "Finlaggan / An Caibeal / The Chapel. Straight ahead of you is the ruin of the 14th century chapel built by John I, Lord of the Isles. A carved stone commemorative cross (*top left*) was discovered in the graveyard next to the chapel. The graveslabs found here include one with an anvil (probably from the grave of a smith), a child's slab (*below left*) and a fine effigy of a man in Highland armour (*far left*) with an image of his galley beneath his feet. This was Donald MacGill-uisbeag (MacIllaspy) who held Finlaggan in the mid-1500's [sic]. The chapel was dedicated to St Findlugan, a monk who came to Scotland during the 6th century when St Columba was also alive. Recent excavations show that some of the burials in the graveyard are of an earlier date than the chapel."

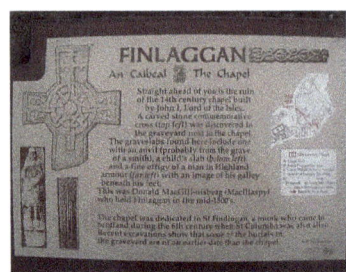
Plaque at Finlaggan

Robert II and Elizabeth Mure

#99 John Mor Tanister MacDonald

John Mor, born in 1360, was the second son of John and Margaret. His father left him a grant of 120 merklands* in Kintyre, with several castles, and 60 merklands in Islay, which included the castle of Dunyvaig. He wasn't satisfied with these inheritances, however, so in 1387 he revolted against his older brother Donald, who had become Lord of the Isles upon their father's death. The revolt lasted until 1395, but even with the support of the MacLeans, John Mor lost and had to retreat to Ireland. There he joined in an alliance with King Richard II of England, until that king was deposed by Henry IV.

In 1399, John married Margery Bisset, daughter of Sir Hugh MacEoin Bisset, Lord of the Glens, and his wife Sabina O'Neill (daughter of Aodh Reamhar O'Neill, King of Ulster).* She was heiress of the Seven Glens of Antrim. Through this marriage, Clan Donald was able to lay claim to the Glens, which Margery's family had established in the previous century. Their son was Donald Balloch MacDonald.

Here we need to pause for a moment to understand the difference between the McDonalds and their chief rivals, the Campbells (Old French *camp belle*, meaning "beautiful fields"). Both clans were Celtic Gaels or Scots, but the ancestors of the Campbells intermarried with Britonic Celts, whereas the ancestors of the Donalds intermarried with the Norse and Vikings.

The two clans had more similarities than differences. For example, the Campbells traditionally married an heiress of the O'Duibne family on Lochawe, who were of a Dalriadic rather than a Pictish origin. However, Angus Mor MacDonald (#96) did the same thing. The root cause of the conflicts between Campbells and Donalds lay in their loyalty or disloyalty to the Kings of Scots.

Clan Campbell was loyal to the Kings of Scots, beginning with Robert the Bruce. When the Stewart kings came to power, the Campbells cemented their loyalty mainly by marrying their daughters into the royal house.

The basis of power of Clan Donald was built by Somerled, who wrested control of the Isles from the Norwegian kings by creating an effective defense force against them. When Somerled died in 1163, his eldest son Dougall retained seniority over Clan Donald. However, the clan Donald began to be weakened due to differing branch clan alliances, religion and geography. Relations were further complicated by alliances with the king of England. It was under these conditions that John Mor was assassinated by James Campbell in Ard Dubh, Islay, Scotland, in 1427.

Campbell, who was attending a meeting there, protested that King James I of Scotland ordered him to do it. A court found that the King had indeed sent Campbell to arrest John Mor, but he over-stepped his authority in killing him. The court found Campbell guilty of murder and hanged him.

* One merkland = 8 ouncelands; 1 ounceland = 20 pennylands.

The Campbells and the McDonalds

When Angus Mor died between 1292 and 1300, Alasdair inherited Islay and part of Knapdale, while Angus Og was left most of Kintyre and a claim to the Isle of Mull, although the latter was still in the hands of their cousins of Clan Dougall. Angus Og was the nephew of Sir Neil Cambel of Lochawe (his mother's brother).

Angus Og's elder brother Alasdair Og married his cousin, the sister of the MacDougall of Lorne. Through this marriage, he was obliged to oppose Robert the Bruce because Bruce had murdered their kinsman, the Red Comyn. However Angus Og, after supporting the English in 1301, joined Sir Neil Campbell in assisting the Bruce as he escaped through Argyll in 1306. On his return journey from Rathlin in 1307, Angus provided men for an unsuccessful attempt to re-capture the Bruce lands in Arran.

After Robert Bruce and his allies defeated MacDougall, Lord of Lorne, at the Battle in the Pass of Brander in 1308, he then laid siege to Alasdair Og MacDonald in Castle Sween. Alasdair gave himself up and was disinherited by Robert Bruce, who then granted Islay to Angus Og. We do not know whether Angus Og and the Campbell knights had been with the Bruce at the Battle of the Pass of Brander, but their presence as his allies seems highly likely. Certainly both Angus Og and his Campbell cousins benefited extensively from the downfall of Clan Dougall following the battle.

Clan Dougall's loss to Robert the Bruce at the Battle of the Pass of Brander began the rise to power of the Bruce's allies, Clan Campbell and Clan Donald.

From Donald Balloch to Sir Daniel

#100 Donald Balloch MacDonald

Donald Balloch MacDonald was born in 1407 at Dunnyveg, Islay, Argyll, Scotland. He was the son of John Mor and Margery Byset. Donald became chief of Clan MacDonald of Dunnyveg after his father was murdered by James Campbell in 1427.

In revenge, Donald defeated the forces of King James I at the battle of Inverlochy in 1431. After a number of subsequent defeats against royal forces, Donald was forced to flee to Ireland. His friend, the Irish Chief Hugh Buy O'Neill, took a pickled head to King James I, claiming it was the head of the rebel Lord Donald. After King James I died, Donald returned to Dunnyveg in 1437.

During his lifetime Donald had three wives: Amicia More; Marie (Mariota) Leslie, daughter of Walter Leslie and Euphemia I, Countess of Ross; Joanna, daughter of Conn O'Neill (b. 1370) and Alice Fitzgerald. By Joanna O'Neill he had three children: Margaret Balloch, who married Roderick MacDonald; Mary, who married Conn O'Neill, Lord of Clandeboye (1445-1482); and John Mor, who married (first) Isabel Campbell and (second) Sabina O'Neill. Donald died on an islet upon Loch Gruinart, Islay, in about 1476.

The Battle of Bloody Bay

Shortly after Donald Balloch's death, the Battle of Bloody Bay was fought (1480-83). This battle was fought between John MacDonald, 4th Lord of the Isles, and his rebellious son Angus Og.

It seems that John had made a secret treaty to help King Edward IV of England invade mainland Scotland. King James III of Scotland stripped John of his earldom and sheriffdoms, but he decreed the title Lord of the Isles would thenceforth be granted by the crown, rather than self-assumed. Many of John's kinsfolk were displeased and wanted to remove John from leadership. Humiliated by the loss of his clan's prestige, his illegitimate son Angus Og ejected John both from the leadership of the clan and from his own home, forcing him to seek shelter under an old boat.

A fierce sea battle took place, turning the waters off the Isle of Mull red. John had the backing of the MacLeans, the MacLeods and the MacNeils. Angus had the support of the MacDonalds of Clan Ranald, Sleat and Keppoch, as well as the MacLeods of Lewis Island. Their chief, William Dubh MacLeod, was killed early on, but a priest ordered the Fairy Flag* to be unfurled. The MacLeods of Lewis then switched to John MacDonald's side. Angus Og won the battle and became the last of the Lord of the Isles. Some believe this battle was the beginning of the end of the clan system. Angus Og was murdered by his harpist Diarmait MacCairbre in 1490 after the title Lord of the Isles transferred to the Scottish Crown. (Diarmait was executed for his crime.)

* The Fairy Flag of the MacLeods

The Fairy Flag, a banner made of yellow or brown silk, is sacred to the MacLeods. It is associated with Celtic fairies and has magical properties, such as multiplying the clan's military forces, saving the lives of certain clan-folk, curing a plague on cattle, increasing fertility, and bringing herring into the loch at Dunvegan. There are two different stories on the origins of the Flag.

One account tells how it was given to the MacLeods by Titania, wife of Oberon, king of the fairies. Titania blessed the flag with magical powers, but they could only be used three times. After that, the flagbearer would be carried off, never to be seen again. According to manuscripts, the Fairy Flag was unfurled at the Battle of Bloody Bay (1480-83) and the Battle of Glendale (1490).

By another account, the Fairy Flag was obtained by a Crusader named MacLeod. Coming home, he attempted to cross a dangerous mountain pass on the border of Palestine. A hermit warned him of a dangerous spirit that guarded the pass, but with a piece of the True Cross, MacLeod defeated the spirit, called the Daughter of Thunder. Before dying, the spirit asked MacLeod to convey some secret to her friends in Scotland. In exchange, she gave him her girdle, which he converted to a banner. He used his spear as a flag pole.

There is a prophecy about the Flag, made by Kenneth Mackenzie, a predictor of the future who lived in the 17th century. When the third Norman Macleod, or son of a hard-boned English lady, perishes by accident, when the Maidens of Macleod (well-known rocks on the coast of Skye) become the property of a Campbell, when a fox bears kits in the turrets of the Dunvegan Castle, and when the Flag should be exhibited for the last time, then the glory of the MacLeods should depart. A great part of their estate should be sold to others, and a small boat would carry all gentlemen named Macleod across Loch Dunvegan, but in the future another John Breac should arise, and will redeem those estates and raise the powers and honor of the house higher than ever.

One Norman MacLeod related how he as a child had talked to an English smith employed at Dunvegan. The smith told him that the chest containing the flag would soon be opened. Around this time (1800) the heir to the chiefship, Norman, was killed when HMS Queen Charlotte caught fire and exploded. About the same time MacLeod's Maidens were sold to the Campbells of Ensay (Ewe Island, in the Outer Hebrides). He also saw a fox with cubs living in the west turret of the castle. (How about the boat full of gentlemen?)

#101 John Mor MacDonald

Born in Ireland in 1445, John Mor was the 3rd chief of Clan MacDonald of Dunnyveg. He became chief when his father Donald Balloch died in 1476. In 1461 he and his father had signed the Treaty of Ardtornish, which divided Scotland between King Edward IV of England and James Douglas, last of the Black Earls.

In 1493 John of Islay (4th Lord, 1434-1503) had to forfeit his title of Lord of the Isles to King James IV of Scotland, and the King took over Dunaverty Castle the following year. Sir John Mor retook Dunaverty Castle just as the King was sailing for Stirling. The King declared Sir John Mor a traitor and summoned him to Edinburgh. Sir John ignored the summons and remained at Islay. However, his kinsman John Maclan of Ardnamurchan betrayed him and he was captured.

John Mor, his son John Cathanach (#102), and his grandsons John Mor, John Og and Donald Balloch were tried for treason and hanged on the Burgh Muir in 1499. John Cathanach's only remaining son Alexander Carragh fled to Ireland. During his life, Sir John Mor married Isabel Campbell first, then Sabina (Sarah) O'Neill, daughter of Felim Bacach O'Neill of Clandeboy.

#102 Sir John Cathanach MacDonald

John Cathanach MacDonald was born in 1465 in Antrim, Ireland. He was the son of John Mor MacDonald and Sabina O'Neill.

When his father John Mór (#101) refused to surrender to King James IV of Scotland, John Cathanach was captured along with his father and brothers. All were tried, convicted of treason and hanged on the Boroughmuir (now Burgh Muir, south of Edinburgh*) in 1499. (His youngest brother Alexander had fled to Ireland and thus became the next head of the lineage.)

While he was still alive, Sir John married Cecilia (Sheela) Savage, daughter of Robert Savage, Lord of the Ardes in Ireland. Their son was Alexander Carragh Macdonald (#103).

* The Burgh Muir was part of the ancient Forest of Drumselch, used for hunting and described as originally an abode of "hartis, hindis, toddis [foxes] and siclike maner of beastis." The Gallow Green was deliberately placed near the road to deter highway robbers. In 1563 a horse thief was hanged there; in 1585 two men were hanged for stealing plague-infected clothing; between 1603 and 1624, thirty-eight members of the outlawed McGregor Clan were hanged [not for playing bagpipes – bearing the name MacGregor was punishable by death]; in 1611, four Gypsies were hanged there, because they were in violation of a parliamentary act banning "Egyptianis." Eleven more Gypsies were hanged in 1624, and their wives sentenced to drown, but instead they were eventually deported.

#103 Alexander Carragh MacDonald
5th of Dunnyveg

Alexander was born in Ulster, Ireland, in 1478, a son Sir John Cathanach and Cecilia Savage. After his father and brothers were executed in 1499, Alexander fled to Ireland. In 1532, he and a force of Gallóglaigh fought the English in Ireland. In 1538, Alexander died at Stirling while on a visit to King James V of Scotland and is buried there.

His first wife was Catherine MacCahalan, daughter of William MacIain. His second wife, also named Catherine, was the daughter of John Macdonald of Ardnamurchan and Helen Campbell. They had eleven children:

Donald MacDonnell was born blind. James MacDonnell of Duniveg and the Glens married Agnes Campbell, daughter of Colin Campbell. James died while imprisoned near Strathbane, Ireland, in 1565. Angus MacDonnell was killed during the Battle of Glentasie in 1565. Colla MacDonnell married Evelyin MacQuillan. Sorley Boy MacDonnell (#104, see below) died in 1590. Alistair Og MacDonnell was killed in 1566. Their other children were named Donald Gorm, Brian Carrach, Ranold Og, Meve and Mary.

K. James V of Scotland

#104 Somhairle Buighe (Sorley Boy) MacDonnell

Somhairle Buighe MacDonnell (pronounced Sorley Boy) was born in 1505, the son of Alexander Carragh and Catherine, his second wife. Based on John Mor Tanister's marriage with Margery Bisset (see #99, above), Sorley Boy claimed lordship of the Glynns in Ireland. Threatened by King James IV of Scotland, the MacDonnells began migrating to Ireland. The English under King Henry VIII were also planning to take over Ulster, and they feared that the O'Neills and O'Donnells (Irish MacDonnells) might welcome a Scottish invasion of Ireland.

When Elizabeth became Queen of England in 1559, she focused on driving a further wedge between the MacDonnells and the O'Neills. Complicating matters were the marriages of chief Shane O'Neill (first) with Catherine MacDonald, daughter of James, Lord of the Isles; then (second) Mary O'Donnell; then (third) Catherine MacLean, whom he discussed divorcing in favor of his girlfriend Agnes Campbell, widow of James MacDonald, whom he had captured at the Battle of Glentasie. Sorley Boy married Mary O'Neill (daughter of Conn O'Neill), Shane's half-sister.

Sorley Boy was a brilliant strategist, delicately balancing relations, through courage, skill and deception, with successive Tudor and Stuart dynasties in England and Scotland. Largely due to his efforts, the MacDonald clan's fortunes were secured and their claims accepted. However, in the years to come, King James VI of Scotland (who became King James I of England) effected the colonization of Northern Ireland in what became known as the Plantation of Ulster, 1610.

With his first wife Mary O'Neill, Sorley Boy had eleven children. His fourth son Randal became Earl of Antrim. When he was eighty-three years old, he married a daughter of Turlough Luineach O'Neill, who was related to Mary. He died in 1590 at Dunanynie Castle.

The Eigg Massacre: MacDonald vs MacLeod

In 1577, the MacDonalds banished three young men of the MacLeod Clan from Eigg, an island off Lochaber, after they insulted (which is to say, they became overly amorous towards) several women. They bound the men hand and foot and cast them to sea in their boat. After the men washed up at Dunvegan, the MacLeods sailed to Eigg to avenge their kinsmens' rude treatment.

The MacDonalds planned to hide in the Cave of Frances. This almost worked, until a watchman's footprints were found and traced back to the cave, whose entrance was obscured by moss, under-growth, and a small waterfall. The MacDonalds thought the cave's narrow entrance would conceal them. However, the MacLeods diverted the waterfall and lit a fire at the cave entrance. The island's entire MacDonald population (more than 350 souls) died from smoke inhalation.

Eleven years later in 1588, some Spaniards who had survived the Spanish Armada found refuge with the MacLeans, who enlisted them in their ongoing feud against the MacDonalds.

#105 Sir James MacDonnell

Following Sorley Boy's death in 1590, his third son James became captain of the Route and part of the Glens of Antrim under his cousin Angus, who was head of the Ian Mor Clan. Almost immediately the MacQuillans tried to forcefully recover the lands they had previously held the MacDonnells displaced them. Both sides appealed, but the government favored the MacQuillans.

This drove a wedge between James and Angus, for Angus didn't want to alienate the English. James was left isolated. James's strategy involved placing the Irish interests of the MacDonnells before their Scottish interests, which was correct, as their true power base lay in Ireland. Over the next decade he displayed considerable skill, both military and diplomatic, in establishing the primacy of the MacSorleys (sons of Sorley Boy) in north-east Ulster. However, Angus landed in Ireland in May 1593 and imprisoned him. James's defiance of the government had been sponsored by Hugh O'Neill, 2nd earl of Tyrone. Tyrone soon compelled Angus to release James.

In August 1596 James took the Glens back from Angus, taking advantage of his cousin's temporary weakness in Scotland after King James VI decided to launch a campaign against him. Happy to keep the MacDonnells divided, the king invited James to Edinburgh, where he knighted him and granted him land.

James remained loyal to the Scottish crown, but for the moment he was dependent on Tyrone. His friendship with the king of Scotland gave him some leverage with Tyrone, who hoped to recruit mercenaries in Scotland. In December 1597, James travelled once more to Edinburgh, where he was warmly received by the king. Nonetheless, as the military tide turned against him, he began once more to court the English. Matters became more complicated when Sir Arthur Chichester was appointed as governor of Carrickfergus in January 1600. Negotiations with the English, which began later that year, progressed slowly. Close to reaching an agreement, James died under extremely suspicious circumstances in April, 1601. James's surgeon was bribed by a Scottish agent to bring about his death. The English government judged that James and Chichester would never cooperate and decided that the simplest solution was to assassinate James, believing that his brother Randal would be easier to get along with. They were wrong.

James' first wife was Mary Margaret O'Neill, daughter of Phelim O'Neill of Clandeboye (another one, not Sabina's father) and Siobhan O'Donnell. They had nine sons. In 1597-98 he was engaged to Alice, Hugh O'Neill's (the Earl of Tyrone's) daughter, who would only have been 9 years old at the time. Alice later married James' brother Randall MacSorley (according to Hugh's will). James was succeeded by his eldest son, Alistair Carragh. A younger son named Sorley was obliged to flee Ireland for conspiring against the crown, eventually finding refuge and a military command in the Spanish army in Flanders.

#106 Alexander Alasdair MacDonnell
1st Baronet of Eanagh

Alexander Alistair MacDonnell was born in Antrim, Ireland, in 1580. His father was Sir James MacDonnell (#105); his mother was Mary O'Brien. (O'Neill?)

The Tudor conquest of Ireland began in the 1540s under Henry VIII and continued into the reign of his daughter Elizabeth I. The *Annals of the Four Masters* records that the land was taken from the Irish and given to foreign tribes, and the Irish chiefs were banished. Alexander was arrested in 1615 for his part in planning an uprising against the Ulster Plantation colonists. He was later released and assigned the newly created title of First Baronet of Eanagh, Ireland, a title that was forfeited in 1691. (One of his sons was obliged to flee Ireland for participating in the 1615 conspiracy, eventually finding refuge and a military command in the Spanish army in Flanders.)

Alexander married Evelyn Magennis (1601-1663), daughter of (Viscount) Arthur Magennis (raised to the peerage in 1623) and Sarah O'Neill. They had six children: Sarah, Rose, Randal, Seumas, James Archibald (#107) and Alexander, 3rd Earl of Antrim (see Siege of Derry, p. 113).

Alexander died in Ireland in 1634.

#107 Sir James Archibald MacDonnell
2nd Baronet

Sir James Archibald MacDonnell was born in Cork, Ireland, in 1615. He later married Mary Penelope O'Brien (1615-1675), daughter of Daniel O'Brien and Ellen Fitzgerald. They had six sons and three daughters, including Sarah, who married Francis (Echlin) Stafford. Their sons were name Daniel, James, and Alexander.

Sir James died in Antrim, Ireland, after 1688.

Arms of MacDonnell of Antrim

#108 Sir Daniel MacDonnell

Born in Antrim, Ireland in about 1640, Daniel MacDonnell was the fourth child of Sir James Archibald MacDonnell and Mary Penelope O'Brien. Deprived of his patrimony in Antrim, Daniel settled at Kilkee, county Clare, where he obtained leases of several lands from his kinsman Lord Clare. His occupation there was gamekeeper for the Lord of Ennis Castle. He married Lady Auberie "Anne" Penelope O'Brien (she later married Henry Howard, 6th Earl of Suffolk). She's the mother of Sir John McDaniel.

Sir Daniel died in 1675 in Clare, Ireland.

I suspect that many of the McDonalds began to move to America (and change or alter their names) after they lost Dunnyveg Castle to the Campbells in 1615.

Table 9a. Beginnings of the O'Neill and O'Cahan Clans

```
Fergaile macMaele Duin High King of Ireland 665-722 ──┬── Aithiochta ingen Cein 670-
                                                      │
              ┌───────────────────────────────────────┴───────────────────────┐
              │                                                               │
Eithne ingen Breasal 730-768 ── Niall Condail MacFergal 718-778    Conchobhar (Buchanan) O'Cathain 720-773
              │                                                               │
       Aedh Oirdnide mac Neill 750-819 ── Maeahbd Inreachtach        Gruagan O'Cathain 772-
              │
Gormlaith ingen Donnchad 792-861 ── Niall Caille mac Aedh 791-846
              │
              │           104 Alpin Dungal macEchdach 778-834
              │                          │
              │           105 Kenneth (Cinead) MacAlpin King of Picts 810-858 ── Miss Leinster 814-
              │                          │
              │                          │                                    Dungan O'Cathain 840-
       Aedh Findliath mac Niall "White Hair" 820-879 ── Mael Muire MacAlpin ingen Cinead 842-913
              │                                                               │
Gormflaith ingen Flann Sinna 870-948 ── Niall mac Aedo 845-919        Cathan (Buchanan) O'Cathain 885-
              │                                                               │
                                                                      Cathusach (Buchanan) O'Cathain 925-

       to Unknown Spouses                                              to Unknown Spouses
```

107

Table 9b. The O'Neills and O'Cahans, leading to John McDonald, Lord of the Isles

The following persons' spouses are unknown:

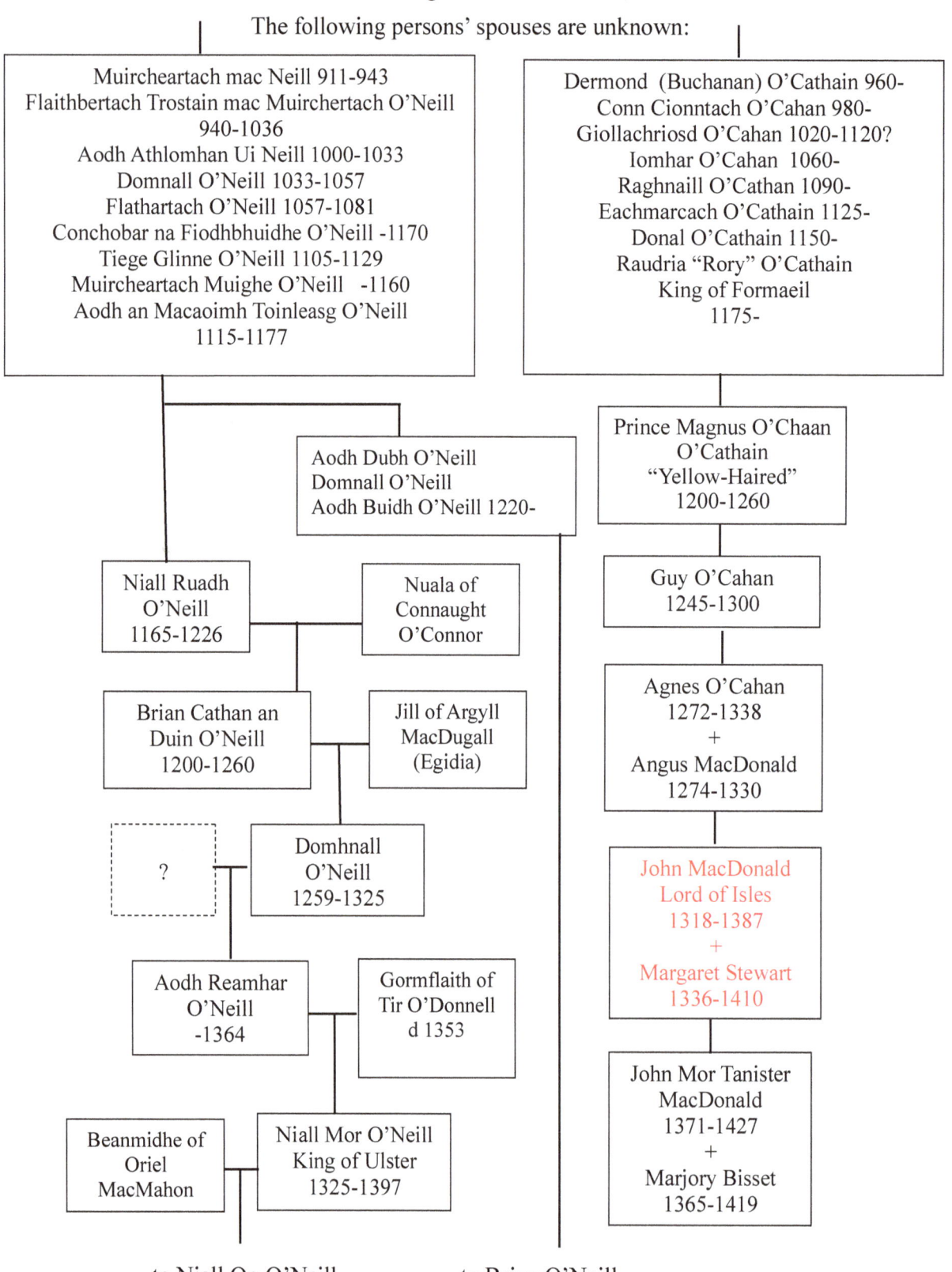

Table 9c. Early Ancestors of Mary O'Neill, and Their Connection to the MacDonalds
from Niall Mor O'Neill   from Aodh Buidh O'Neill

- Niall Og O'Neill 1345-1403 — Una O'Neill dtr of another Domnall
- Brian O'Neill 1235-
- Henry O'Neill 1290-1347
- Muircheartach -1395
- Brian O'Neill 1370-1425
- Aedh Buidhe O'Neill

- Conn (I) Baccach? O'Neill 1370-1444 — Alice ? FitzGerald 1380-
- Joanna O'Neill 1410-1485 — Donald MacDonald 1407-1476 2nd Dunnyveg
- Catherine MacMahon — Eoghan Mor O'Neill King of Ulster -1456
- Mary MacDonald 1450-1488 — Conn O'Neill 1444-1482
- Henri mac Eoghain O'Neill 1415-1490
- Sabina O'Neill 1423-1470 — John Mor MacDonald 1425-1499
- Joan Cam — Thom. FitzGerald d. 1478
- John Cathanach MacDonald 1435-1499 + Sheela Cecila Savage
- Gerald 'Mor' FitzGerald 1456-1513
- Eleanor Fitzgerald 1450-1497 — Conn Mor O'Neill 1468-1493
- Alexander Carragh MacDonald d. 1538 + Catherine MacCahalan
- Conn II mac Cuinn O'Neill 1480-1559 1st Earl of Tyrone — Alice (Alison) Fitzgerald 1480 – (or dtr O'Byrne)
- Mary O'Neill 1515-1590 (Poss. Illegit.) — Somhairle Buidhe MacDonnell 1505-1590

109

Table 9d. Descendants of Mary O'Neill; Ancestors of Rebecca Williams

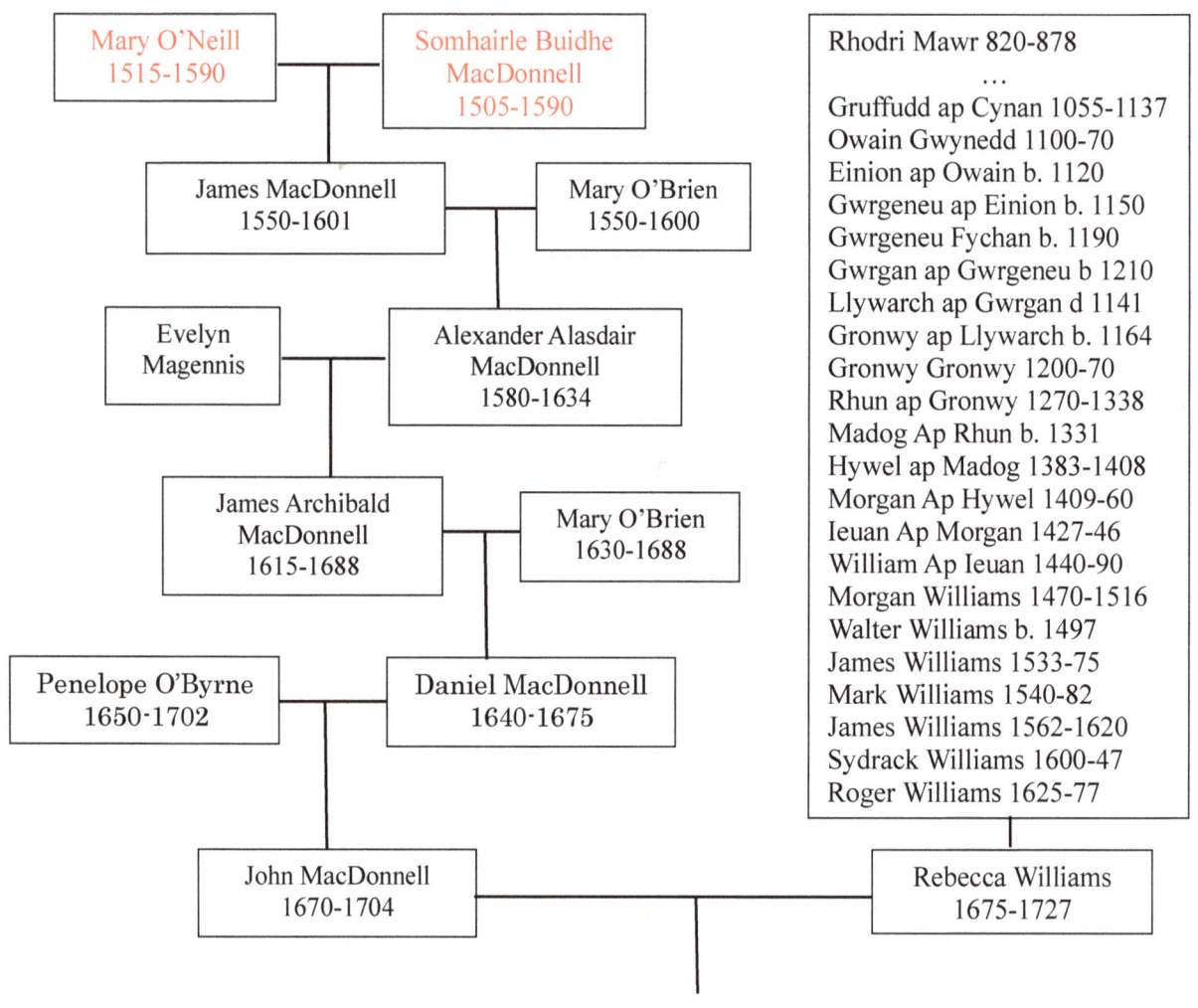

The Glencoe Massacre

The MacDonalds had historically gotten along rather well with the Campbells, but then in the late sixteenth century, relations began to sour. The MacDonalds of Glencoe sometimes engaged in piracy in the narrow waters of the lochs. They had a practice of painting their galleys white on one side and black on the other so that those seeing them going would not recognize them when returning laden with spoils. Glencoe claimed they did not join in these expeditions, but as the Campbells rose to power, the Glencoe Donalds began to take part in the pirate raids.

Things culminated with the 1692 massacre at Glencoe. The massacre was planned in London and Edinburgh, masterminded by John Dalrymple, Master of Stair, the Secretary of State over Scotland and Lord Advocate. The killings were carried out by the English army under the orders of King William III.

England had demanded that the Scots submit to them no later than 1691. Alexander, 12th Chief of the Clan, was old and did not understand the gravity of the situation. He tried to take the oath of allegiance at Fort William, which was a long way to go from the Pass of Glencoe in winter.

When he returned, Alexander told his people he had taken the oath, but the authorities took no account of it. The order was given January 11 for a general massacre. William III of Orange, King of England, spoke no English, and the Master of Stair, a Campbell, Secretary for Scotland, concealed Alexander's submission was concealed from the king.

The government troops in Glencoe had been blamed for turning upon their hosts and committing murder. The troops had not been invited into Clan Donald homes at all, but were forcibly quartered with them as punishment for failure to pay property taxes.

On January 16, the Master of Stair cut off all retreat from the Pass of Glencoe, ordering every MacDonald in Glencoe under seventy to be executed, making sure that "the old fox [Alexander] and his cubs should be put to death."

Captain Robert Campbell of Glenlyon was in the army because he had recently been bankrupted; his family was destitute. Captain Campbell bore no ill will towards the MacDonalds of Glencoe in spite of the fact that in 1689 the MacIains of Glencoe, together with their cousins the MacDonnells of Glengarry, looted Glenlyon, stole his livestock, and razed Campbell's last remaining holdings. In his appeal for compensation, Campbell showed he clearly believed the Glengarry men should be held responsible, not those of Glencoe. While quartered at Glencoe, Captain Campbell stayed at the home of Alexander MacDonald, MacIain's youngest son, who was married to Campbell's niece, the sister of Rob Roy MacGregor. He even played cards with Alastair.

However, Capt. Campbell's superior officers had made severe threats were made against him, just a few hours before the killings. If he failed to order the killings, he would be accused of treason for which the punishment was death. At 4:00 a.m. on February 1, a shot rang out and all hell broke loose. The Chief (Alexander) was shot thru the head. His wife's jewels were pulled off, her rings torn from her fingers with teeth, and she died the next day. Two sons managed to escape by their perfect knowledge of the Pass.

A government piper played a well-known Campbell tune of warning before the massacre ("The Campbells Are Coming"). Many of the MacDonalds escaped over the passes onto Campbell lands where they were sheltered by sympathetic residents. In the end, the massacre was so badly conducted that only thirty-eight of the three hundred MacDonalds in Glencoe were killed, a hint at the unwillingness of the Highlanders to kill their neighbors with whom they had been quartered.

A soldier was ordered to kill any child that was male, but seeing a woman and child hidden among the rocks (it was a boy) he killed a dog instead and showed the blood on his sword as proof. In all 80 were slaughtered, and many more died of exposure. There homes were burned, 1200 cattle and horses and large numbers of sheep and goats were driven to Fort William.

The Master of Stair was finally blamed, and ended his life by suicide in 1707.

The Glencoe Massacre

Part 7
The Americans

The MacDonalds were highly loyal to Scotland and rallied to the support of both the Old Pretender James Francis Edward Stuart (son of James II), and to Bonnie Prince Charley (Charles Edward Stuart), the Young Pretender. After they Highlanders were conquered, between 1763-1775 no fewer than 20,000 Highlanders sought refuge in America. Their names are Donald, Donnell, Donnellson, Donaldson, MacDonald, McDonnell etc. Many went to Ireland.

The Siege of Derry

When the Glorious Revolution overthrew King James II, replacing him with William of Orange, James fled to France where he was protected by King Louis XIV, who had persecuted the Huguenots, sending refugees to northern Europe (and America). Meanwhile William and Mary were offered the Scottish throne. Ireland was still ruled by the Earl of Tyrconnel, appointed by James in 1687. He was from an Old English Catholic family and had replaced Protestant officers in the army with Catholic ones.

James ordered Alexander MacDonnell* (1615-1699), Earl of Antrim (a Catholic) to raise a regiment in Ulster. Alexander hired 1,200 Scottish "redshank" mercenaries, all Catholics. One Irish unit that remained Protestant was still garrisoned at Derry. James ordered MacDonnell's regiment to replace them. When MacDonnell tried to cross under Derry's Ferryquay Gate (December, 1688), thirteen apprentice boys seized the city keys and locked the gates.

In April, 1689, James himself came with an Irish army led by Jacobite and French officers and laid siege to the town. The townspeople by that time had shifted their allegiance, and refused to surrender. They shot a cannon called "Roaring Meg" at the king, killing his aide-de-camp. However, ships carrying supplies arrived: HMS *Dartmouth*, *Mountjoy*, *Phoenix* and *Jerusalem*, and unloaded tons of food. They broke through, so they lifted the siege.

"That the influence of the MacDonnells was widespread in Ireland can be gleaned from the fact that the attainder of 1642 included six MacDonnells in County Wicklow, three in County Cork, two in Dublin and one in Kildare. The Outlaweries of 1691 included Six MacDonnells of Antrim, four of Mayo, two of Leitrim and one each in the counties of Roscommon and Clare."

* Son of Randal (4th son of Sorley Boy); seventy-three years old at the time.

Table 10. The Americans

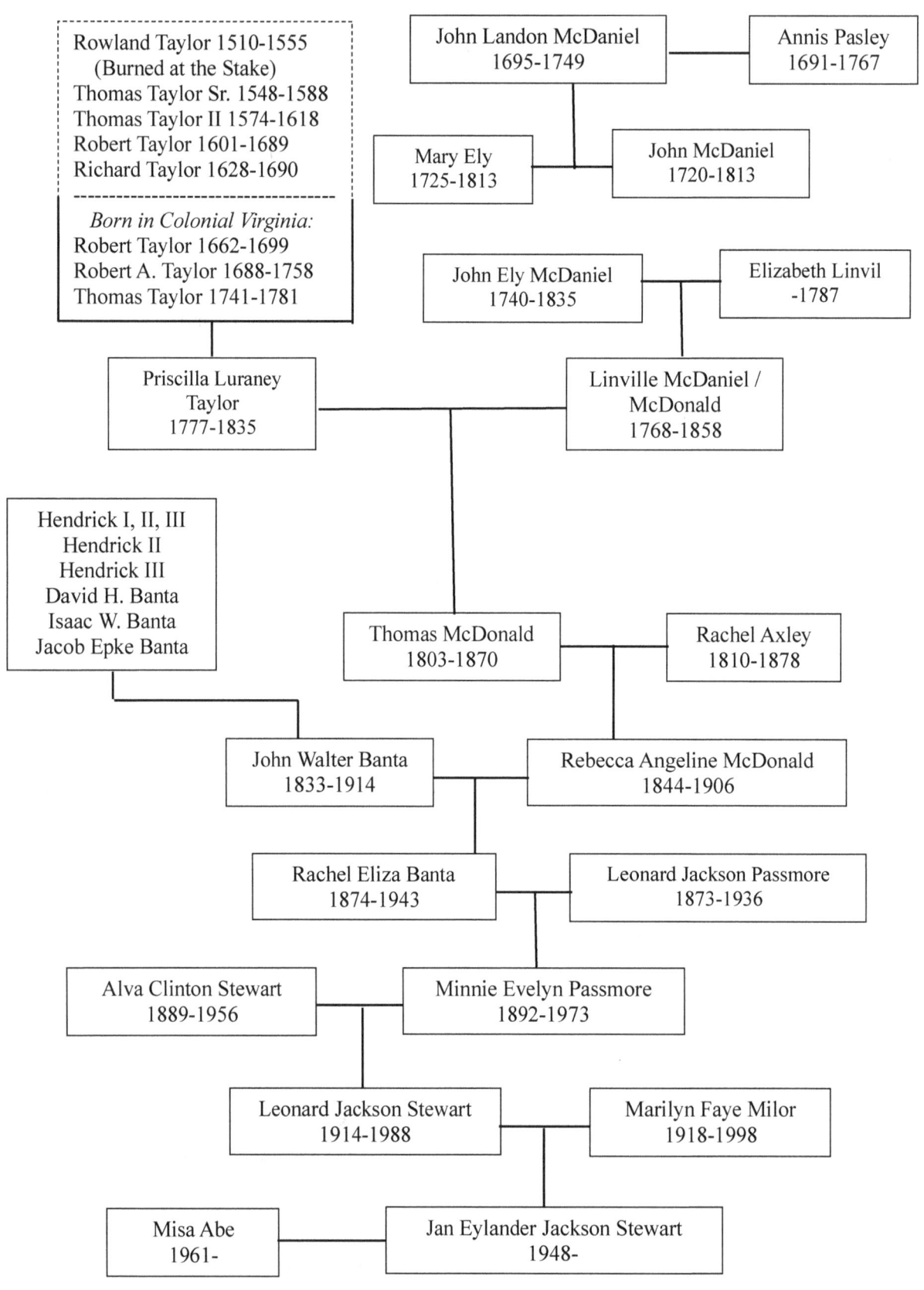

From Sir John MacDonnell to Jan Stewart

#109 Sir John MacDonnell

John MacDonnell was born in 1670 in Munster, Ireland. His father was Sir Daniel MacDonnell. His mother was Lady Auberie O'Brien. He was (also) Game Keeper for the Lord of Ennis Castle.

In about 1690 he emigrated to Virginia.

During his lifetime he had at least four wives: Joan, Susannah, Sarah Jones, and Rebecca Brooke Williams (1675-1727), whom he married in Wise, Virginia, in 1696. John and Rebecca had a son named John Landon McDaniel.

Sir John was killed by Indians in Virginia, 1704. After that, Rebecca married a second husband, George Thompson I, with whom she had second son, George William Thompson II.

Here is the Will left by Nathaniel FRITH or THRIFT [Rebecca's grandfather], dated: 04 July 1677 which mentioned ...

> - to sons Nathaniel & William Frith, my plantation which I now live on and the land belonging to it which is in all 150 acres, to be equally divided betwixt them and if one dies the other to have it all.
> - to wife Elizabeth [née Parsons] all my moveables & cattle saving only one cow calf to be delivered to my goddaughter [= granddaughter] **Rebecca Williams**, daughter of Jone [née Frith] Williams.

Whereas Nathaniell FRITH did by his last Will give to **Rebecca WILLIAMS**, a cow calfe, in ye behalf thereof, ye said Rebeccah WILLIAMS, I, the subscriber, Samll. WELLS, doe desire that ye said calfe may be recorded for ye use of the said Rebeccah, with all female increase forever, ye male to remaine to those yt: shall looke after the said cow calfe until ye said Rebeccah WILLIAMS is of age [she was only two years old in 1677]; ye said calfe is marked with, a crop & slitt in ye right eare & a crop & hole in ye left eare.

#110 John Landon McDaniel, Sr.

John Landon McDaniel was born in 1695 in Virginia. His father was Sir John MacDonnell, and his mother was Rebecca Williams (1675-1727), daughter of Roger Williams (not the same as the historical figure, see Table 9d, page 107). His maternal grandmother was Mrs. Joanne Frith (1646-1703), the widow of Samuel Willis (married in 1667), who married Roger Williams in 1669. She later married Lewis Lloyd in 1684.

In 1720, John McDaniel married Annis Pasley,* daughter of Robert John Pasley and Eleanor McLean. Their children were John Jr., George, Henry, Jeremiah, and William Joel.

John McDaniel died about 1749, and is buried at North Farnham Episcopal Church Cemetery, Farnham, Virginia.

After John died, his widow Annis married Phillip Webber (1690-1761), with whom she had three children: Augustine, Mary Elizabeth and Phillip Jr.

#111 John Landon McDaniel Jr.

John Landon McDaniel Jr. was born on October 22, 1720, in Richmond, Virginia. His father was John Landon McDaniel, and his mother was Annis Pasley.

In 1740, he married Mary Polly Ely (1725-1763) and had these children: John Ely McDonald (b. 1740), Major Eli Pasley McDaniel (b. 1742), William McDaniel (b. 1744), James (b. 1746) Sarah McDaniel (b. 1746), McDaniel (b. 1748), Daniel Thomas McDaniel (b. 1750), Mary (b. 1752), Peter (b. 1763).

He died in 1813, in Chatham, North Carolina, at the age of 93, and was buried in Asbury Methodist Church Cemetery, Chatham County, North Carolina.

* Several websites list a Margaret Eleanor Davis as being John's second wife, but this woman lived much later (1835-1896) and married another John Landon McDaniel (1829-1902), descendant of one Randolph McDaniel, who was born in Ireland in 1734.

#112 John Ely McDonald (McDaniel)

John Ely McDonald was born John McDaniel in Richmond, Virginia in 1740. The surname McDonald started with John (#111) and Mary Polly's children, who went to court to change their surname back to McDonald.

John married Elizabeth Linvil. John and Elizabeth had these children: John McDaniel (b. 1767), Linvil (1768-1858), Eli (b. 1769), Melchi (1771-1830), Robert (b. 1773), and Sarah (b. 1776).

After Elizabeth died (around 1787-88), John married Margaret Watkins. Her son was Rev. Thomas Smith McDaniel.

John died in Jefferson County, Tennessee, in 1835.

In a keynote address* to the National Cowboy Poetry Gathering, 1999, William McDonald claimed "the McDonalds were already in America, they came over in the eighteenth century from the Highlands after the defeat of Bonnie Prince Charlie. I assume that it was time to get out of town, and they were, they clung to the clannish ways of the old country. They landed in North Carolina and kind of moved in a big group of relations from Tennessee to Illinois, winding up, most of them in the Hill Country of Texas, around Fredericksburg."

* The speech was entitled, "A Tradition Worth Keeping." This author harbors doubts about the accuracy of that statement, especially in regards to their moving in a big group of relations, but let's assume that it was more or less true, or at least, that it suited the taste of the cowboys.

#113 Linvil McDonald

Linvil McDaniel was born in 1768, in Orange, North Carolina. His father was John Ely McDaniel, and his mother was Elizabeth Linvil.

He married Priscilla Luraney Taylor about 1796, in Chatham, North Carolina, United States. She was the daughter of Thomas Taylor and Eleanor Dodson. They were the parents of many sons and daughters: Celia, David, James, Eleanor, Thomas, William, Joseph, Elizabeth and John.

At one point, the McDonalds lived in St. Clair, Illinois. Luraney died in 1820. Then in 1835 Linvil married Elizabeth (b. 1783), who went by the nickname "Eliza."

Linvil died in 1858, in Jefferson, Illinois, at the age of 90 and was buried in Ebenezer Cemetery, Rome Township, Jefferson, Illinois, alongside his second wife.

Linvil McDonald

Rowland Taylor

Luraney Taylor was a descendant of Rowland Taylor (1510-1555), who studied law at Cambridge. In 1528 he was ordained as an exorcist and acolyte at Norwich, but for about ten years he worked for the Archdeacon of Ely, focusing on law. He associated himself with Protestant reformers after hearing sermons by Hugh Latimer, Bishop of Worcester. When Latimer resigned, Rowland became chaplain to Thomas Cranmer, Archbishop of Canterbury. Cranmer made him a commissioner for the reform of church laws. Upon the death of King Edward VI, Taylor joined the attempt to secure the throne for Lady Jane Grey. He was arrested in 1553 and imprisoned for several months. After he was freed, Queen Mary I again ordered his arrest, but this time he was accused of denouncing the Pope and opposing the celibacy of priests. He was sentenced to death as a heretic in 1555 and burned at the stake in Suffolk. His wife Margaret's surname was not known, but since his marriage took place in the London home of John Tyndale, she is remembered as Margaret Tyndale.

#114 Thomas McDonald

Thomas McDonald was born on June 4, 1803, in Chatham, North Carolina. His father was Linvil McDaniel / McDonald, and his mother was Priscilla Luraney Taylor.

Thomas married Rachel Axley on June 14, 1827, in Jefferson, Illinois. She was the daughter of Rev. Pleasant David Axley (1775-1818). They had at least four sons and four daughters: Mary Moore, James Monroe, Melvina, Susanna Mariah, Rebecca Angeline, Robert Lafayette "Lafe", William Augustus, and Samuel Thomas.

Thomas and Rachel moved to Gillespie, Texas. Thomas died in 1870 in Spring Creek, at the age of 67, and was buried in Spring Creek Cemetery, Harper, Gillespie County, Texas.

Thomas and his Daughters

Mahala Alwilda McDonald (Lafayette's wife) was staying with her parents, Wylie and Elizabeth Joy (née Frazier) who lived on James Peak, while her husband was away in Old Mexico during the Civil War. (Born in Illinois, he couldn't fathom anyone going to war against the US Government, so he and his friend tried to escape the Confederate army in Mexico.)

Someone had recently brought some letters from Lafe McDonald and left them at the home of his father Thomas McDonald, who lived on Spring Creek, about eight miles east of Harper (the nearest mail delivery was at Fredericksburg). Mahala was anxious to hear from her husband, so she insisted that someone go on horseback with her to Spring Creek. She and her mother saddled their horses, determined to go there and back in one day, but they had to wait until the next morning to return.

The two women crossed Banta Branch Creek, where several Indians (presumed to be Comanches) ambushed them. The mother fell first and lay on the west side of the creek. Alwilda tried to escape on her black horse, but she fell about half a mile from her mother's body on the east side of the creek. Many guessed that this deed was not done by Indians, but moccasin tracks and other savage signs were discovered shortly afterwards. A Texas Ranger came upon a wounded Indian, lying near the edge of the river about fifteen miles west of Harper in Kimble County, and figured he was among the culprits. (A more grizzly account tells that the women were beheaded and sent back home on their buggy.)

#115 Rebecca Angeline McDonald

Rebecca Angeline McDonald was born on February 7, 1844, in Jefferson, Illinois. Her father was Thomas McDonald, and her mother was Rachel Axley.

Rebecca married John Walter Banta on January 20, 1860, in Gillespie, Texas. They were the parents of at least seven sons and four daughters, including Rachel Eliza (#116). She lived in Justice Precinct 4, Bastrop, Texas, and Bandera, Texas. She died on January 9, 1906, in Mason, Texas, at the age of 61, and was buried in Old Gooch Cemetery, Mason, Texas.

The following is an account from the diary (1898) of her son-in-law Leonard Passmore:

Christmas in Texas

"What a beautiful season of the year, 'tis Christmas and all of the family are congregating at John and Angeline Banta's household for the holidays.

"At about 8 P.M. we arrived at father-in-law's home… Old Grandma McDonald, Bro. Banta's mother-in-law*, bowed down with her over 'four score years and ten' [years], was helped into the room to view the tree. The sight would have made a beautiful picture. It pictured frail humanity bowing at the tree of Life to receive the blessed gifts to be bestowed upon the children of the faithful after the resurrection."

* This was John Banta's *mother*, not his mother-in-law. Rebecca's mother, Rachel Axley McDonald [born Sept. 6, 1810], died in 1878, twenty years before this Christmas. Born Eliza Barker in 1806, this "Old Grandma" married Zachariah McDonald after the death of her first husband Isaac Banta.

Interestingly, Rebecca Angeline's brother "Lafe," having run away to Old Mexico to escape the draft, came back across the border, trying to get to Florida. He was caught by the Confederates and forced to join the army. The muster rolls of McCord's Frontier Regiment (East Texas 46th) include not only Private Robert L. McDonald (possibly "L" for Lafayette), but also Private Zachariah McDonald. Not sure if these were the same persons… Eliza's second husband must have been considerably older than "Lafe."

Rebecca and John Banta

Texas Rangers

#116 Rachel Eliza Banta

Rachel Eliza Banta was born in 1874 in Bastrop, Texas. Her father was John Walter Banta, and her mother was Rebecca Angeline McDonald.

In her teen years she went to school at Onion Creek, Texas. Another student in the school was a young, good-looking boy with a quiet, charming manner about him. His name was Leonard Passmore. They were childhood sweethearts. Here is part of a poem by "Babe Bert," his pen name:

> The worms came in the summer
> And devoured the leaves of the pecan trees;
> We wondered if the fruitage abundant,
> Would mature in the autumn and ripen;
> For the nuts, all bare, were left hangin'
> In clusters on the trees that were growing
> Like giants, by the edge of the brooklet.
> To our vision, they appeared more distinctly
> Than if hidden among the green foliage.
> Now is the month of October.
> The myriads of the brown nuts are showing
> And out on the limbs, there are springing
> New leaves, that appear to out rival
> The beauty of those that were destroyed,
> That grew on the trees in the "Springtime."
> (Oct. 30, 1928)

In November, 1891, she married Leonard Passmore at Spring Creek. Their children's names were Minnie Evelyn (b. 1892), Dora Claire (b. 1895), Clarence (b., d. 1897), Angeline Epsy (b. 1897), Epsy Angelyne (b. 1898 m. Mr. Echols), Edith (1900-1901), Claud Merritt (b. 1902), Alma Mae (b. 1904), Leah Violet (b. 1906), and Daymon Slator (b. 1912). Rachel died on 8 May 1943, in Voca, Texas, at the age of 68, and was buried in Voca Cemetery.

Photo of L.J. Passmore, Fourth Row, Far Right (Teacher)

#117 Minnie Evelyn Passmore

Minnie Evelyn Passmore was born in 1892 in Doss, Texas. Her father was Leonard Jackson Passmore, and her mother was Rachel Eliza Banta. She married Alva Clinton Stewart in 1913. They were the parents of three sons: Leonard Jackson, Dorman McMillan, and Othello Merle. She died in 1973, in Brady, Texas, at the age of 80, and was buried in Voca Cemetery.

The Singing Convention

The Singing Convention is a gathering of gospel singers. Minnie and her sons often gathered at our house in the Vineyard in a Cove to renew their spirits. Minnie sang soprano while she played the piano; Old Jack sang alto; Dorman sang tenor; Othello sang in his rich, bass voice.

The Quilting Bee

The photo pictured below (right) is a Friendship Quilt made by the Voca Quilting Club in the early 1950s for Grandmother Lane. Names on the quilt include Nancy Willis, Ruby Liverman, Annie Bodenlomer, Opal Holloway, Grace Holloway, **Evelyn Stewart**, Minnie Brown, Georgia Locklear, **Leah** (Minnie's 'Little Sister'), Mamie Behrens, Winnie Deans, Lina Miller, Lillie Spiller, Ollie Whitley, Betty Deans, and Bertha Schooley.

Little Angie

Angeline Epsy Passmore was named after her two grandmothers. Minnie always wondered why her father doted on Little Angie so much. Perhaps she had blonde hair. Perhaps he simply "connected" with her. Leonard J. Passmore wrote this entry in his *Diary*, January 12, 1900:

> "Beautiful, beautiful childhood, Dearer, oh dearer, than all else to me,
> Would that your pleasures could last; Are the sweet dreams of the past."

Soon after that his diary continued: "But pull aside the curtain and peer into the future a few years. What do we see?" Little Angie died young; another sister was similarly named Epsy Angelyne.

Low-Water Crossing over the San Saba River

Friendship Quilt

#118 Leonard Jackson Stewart

Leonard Jackson Stewart was born in 1914, in Junction, Texas. His father was Alva Clinton Stewart. His mother was Minnie Evelyn Passmore. In 1941 he married Marilyn Faye Milor in Clark, Nevada. They were the parents of four children: Gale Jackson (d. 1941), Diane Jacqueline, Jan Eylander Jackson, and Karen Elaine. He grew up in Brea, California, and graduated from San Jose State College. He worked as a school teacher in California, moving around from Blythe, Santa Ynes, Azusa, and ending up in Covina. He died in Los Angeles in 1988, at the age of 73.

I grew up in the house that Jack built. It was located on Cypress Avenue, in County territory just outside the incorporated city of Covina. The house was built on 2/3 of an acre, carved out of one of those orange groves that blanketed Southern California in the good old days. It was a one-story "ranch house," built in the shape of an L.

The front entrance was at the elbow of the L. Step inside and you were in the "living room," though no one did much living in there, except me. The main family room was accessed through a sliding door, by way of the kitchen-dining room. Going straight down the long corridor from the "living room" would take you to the bedrooms and bathrooms.

They called the main family room the "den." True to the standard of the day, it featured a fireplace and a long turquoise couch that curved around the perimeter of the room. Jack's easy chair held a prominent position in that room.

Back to the "living room." That's where the piano and stereo were, as well as the telephone, so that's where I spent my adolescent days. Old Jack had two little pictures of palm trees in bamboo frames hanging up behind the telephone. I never knew where those pictures were taken (or painted). The image that dominated the room was a picture of a panther that Jack and Faye bought at Sears in downtown Los Angeles. Of course, the cat was black, its eyes shining yellow. It sat in a tree in the middle of a jungle whose leaves receded in various shades of green, darker green, and darkest green, hinting at Conrad's "horror" in the depths beyond.

In the front yard, there was a hump. That's what we called the cesspool. It had to be emptied occasionally, as this house in unincorporated territory did not qualify to join the sewer system. Old Faye planted her flowers out there between the hump and the street. Bougainville flowers grew up near the house.

In the back yard, among the remaining orange trees, lay the horse pen — where old Dolly and Penny dined on oats… I raked — and the swimming pool.

In the way back, Old Jack planted his boysenberry vines. We had stopped beside the road one night out behind Knott's Berry Farm (in those days there were no fences) in Buena Park, and Old Jack kleptoed a few branches from the vines. Then he transplanted them to the "back 40" of his gentleman's farm in Charter Oak, or the Vineyard in a Cove.

When Old Jack died in 1988, the County Board of Supervisors planted a tree in his name.

#119 Jan Eylander Jackson Stewart

Motto (1966-1973): *Vivat! Vivat! Vivat! Academia!* (Live on! Live on! Live on! Academia!)
Motto (1974-1983): *Lyrae Nervos Aptavi* (I Have Tuned the Strings of My Harp)
Motto (1984-Pres.) *Eigo Ergo Sum* (English, Therefore I Am)

Misa's paternal grandfather dropped out of school and went to work as a porter at the train station. There he was "discovered" by the president of Daiai Movie Co., who kidnapped him and took him home. This grandfather became vice president of the company, and eventually, the wealthiest man in Kyushu. Daiei produced Akira Kurosawa's *Rashomon* (1950) and *Gamella*.

It took eight years to learn the truth, the whole truth, and nothing but the truth. Until then, it had to suffice that this grandfather had been shot, poisoned, and thrown off a train in China. What would it take for him to be hated that much? Well, knowing Misa's sister, it was easy to guess, if she took after her grandfather. How a person could spin a half-truth into that much of a sinister lie was almost beyond belief. And what was the whole truth? A clue may be found in the moniker of Misa's father, which was "The Prince of Manchuria."

The Little Prince was the picture of second-generation wealth, all to be squandered in the end. He was not without his own talent, but he lacked the stick-with-it-ivity to make of himself a long-term success. Instead, he used his wealth to impress people and manipulate them, buying himself any number of "beneficiary" friends. Few turned out to be true friends.

As for Misa herself, she is this author's Penelope, from Homer's *Odyssey*. Penelope demonstrates loyalty and faith. Whereas Athena often came to Penelope in dreams to reassure or comfort her, Misa, too, has her dreams. She has a kind of déjà vu talent, in which she sometimes feels that she is living an event for the second time, having dreamed it before (similar to Louise in the 2016 film, *Arrival*). One night she woke me up and said, "I dreamed you were working for a big refrigerator company in Saudi Arabia." I told her that she was crazy and to go back to sleep. Seven years later I found myself working for Raytheon, maker of Gibson refrigerators, in Saudi Arabia.

Virtue and fidelity. Whereas Penelope constantly had to fend off suitors who assumed Odysseus would not return, Misa's suitors sometimes appeared as soon as I had stepped out of the room. I was always befuddled by this. Was marriage so unholy to them? Yet Misa is a child of promise.

Intelligence and cunning. Penelope never refused her suitors outright, but promised to decide once she finished a burial shroud for Odysseus' father, Laertes. Then every evening she undid her day's work, never finishing the shroud. She later announced that she would hold a contest in which the suitors were to be asked to string the great bow of Odysseus and shoot an arrow through a dozen axes, knowing that only her husband could do this. Misa would also use her suitors' weakness against them, in my favor. (What was my "great bow"? What were my "dozen axes"?)

As for Jan, I was not raised in Ithaca. I was raised Arcadia, a land where walnut trees lined streets without curbs. We lived on Mayflower Street. I went to Plymouth School. A real Pilgrim.

As a young man, I prayed to God: "If You are real, please show me." It was not long afterward that a young Jewish boy and a fair Mexican maiden invited me to a devotional concert at St. Lucy's High School for Girls. There I made the transition from a slick-down church Christian (through the cocoon stage of a Lost Sheep, or Prodigal Son) to being a true Christian. In 1970, I was baptized in the Pacific Ocean at Devereaux Beach near Santa Barbara.*

Many times after that I prayed the prayer of Jabez, who called on the God of Israel saying, "Oh, that thou wouldst bless me indeed, and enlarge my coast, and that thine hand might be with me, and that thou wouldst keep me from evil, that it may not grieve me" – I Chron 4:10 (KJV). And God granted me that which I requested: He blessed me with Misa, two children, and many grandchildren. He enlarged my coast, as we have lived at various times in Denver, San Francisco, Spain, Saudi Arabia, and Japan. His hand went with me, as several times an angel stepped in to protect me from accidents. He kept me from evil, which I encountered many times… for pure Evil is a thing to fear, and a thing to avoid at all costs, though it exists in abundance all around us.

I don't remember the name of the book we were discussing, but as we sat in the round-table seminar room at Claremont Graduate School, the class Atheist commented: "I am struck by the overwhelming Christianity of this." I and my fellow Christians had question-mark shaped haloes hovering over our heads at this statement. I challenged him. "If you are overwhelmed by this, I should hope you never read the Bible!"

People sometimes ask me how it is to live in Japan. I always answer: it is the same as any place; there are good people, and there are bad people. The difference is that in Japan (as with the girl with the great big curl right in the middle of her forehead), when they are good, they are very, very good; when they are bad, they are horrid!

In *The Once and Future King*, Avalon was the place King Arthur went when he died, to await his own resurrection. It is also the name of a real town, somewhere west of the City of Angels. As for me, I have journeyed somewhere west of Avalon, to live out my days as a stranger in a strange land, living in a working class utopia somewhat petulantly called Wayward Pines. In that sense, I am *Gaijin Quandam, Gaijin Futuris* ("The Once and Future Foreigner"). Am I truly *Futuris*?

Eternal life is the object of all religions, but is it just a dream? Are we nothing but mold growing on the surface of the planet? I think human life is too complex just to have risen from clay – carbon jigsaw puzzles – quirks of the cosmos. So what is the soul? That is the $64 question.

* David Wilcock, in his painfully detailed autobiography called *The Ascension Mysteries*, tells of a similar experience, though in his case he called out to the Cosmos and was answered by a shooting star. I don't know how he was "baptized."

Conclusion

In this tome we have seen some remarkable lineages, continued without seam. First, the Hebrews from Noah to Darda. Then, the Trojans from Darda to Thor. After that, the Scandinavians from Thor to Odin, "to infinity and beyond." These same Scandinavians then invaded Ireland, beginning with Ivar the Boneless, and they eventually became native Irish, morphing into Scots (as they inhabited the Isles and the Dalriada). These led eventually to Somerled, the "All-father" of Scotland, and specifically, the McDonald Clan.

Coming around from another way, we have the original Irish peoples, who came to the island in waves, through Spain from Scythia.

We have also seen a number of writing systems develop, beginning with the Hebrew, Greek, and Latin alphabets transmitted by Cadmus, brother of Fennius, and including the Ogham alphabet which was used to describe Ancient Irish. Odin, arguably of Hebrew descent, was allowed to "see" the Runes, after making a great sacrifice on *Yggdrasil*, the World Tree. It is in this spirit of passing on knowledge from one generation to the next that I have written, in English letters, the history of the McDonald Clan.

Plato, in *Phaedrus*, gives an anecdote about the relationship between writing and memory. In his story of an ancient Egyptian god named Theuth, who supposedly invented letters, the King of all Egypt at the time was a person named Thamus. Theuth presented his invention to the king, who told him, "… you, as the father of letters, have been led by your affection for them to describe them as having the opposite of their real effect. For your invention will produce forgetfulness in the souls of those who have learned it, through lack of practice at using their memory, as through reliance on writing they are reminded from outside by alien marks, not from within, themselves by themselves. So you have discovered an elixir not of memory but of reminding" (*Phaedrus*, page 275a, transl. by Christopher Rowe).

So I leave you with this "big huge" reminder, in the words of King Thamus (who brazenly one-upped the god Theuth), of all those men and women who went before us, if we happen to spring from that well that is called McDonald. Incidentally, I have thrown in a few nice "O's" for good measure, giving due credit to the Irish side of what has otherwise been remembered as an exclusively Scottish name.

Well, nothing is exclusively Scottish, not even my own surname (Stewart), which boasts members not only from Scotland, but also from Ireland (that is, emigrants to the Ulster Plantation) as well as from France (don't forget the Seneschals of Dol).

Be ye good stewards of your heritage. In the words of Bob Dylan, "You are a walking antique"!

A Few Notable Mc's

MacArthur (from the Celtic name *Arthur:* 'son of Arthur', which means noble one.)

Douglas MacArthur's great-grandmother Sarah was married to a Mr. MacArthur (we don't know his first name) in Scotland. After her husband died, she married one Alexander Meggett. In 1828 the Meggetts relocated to Uxbridge, Massachusetts, near Sarah's sister. Sarah died in Pawtucket, Rhode Island, and was buried in Slatersville Cemetery, Providence County, Rhode Island.

Sarah's son was Arthur MacArthur Sr., who served as Governor of Wisconsin in 1856. His son, Arthur Jr., was a noted Civil War Union general. Arthur Jr's son was Douglas MacArthur, who became a five-star General in the U.S. Army.

Douglas attended the US Military Academy, West Point, graduating first in his class of 1903. During World War I, he became Major General and commander of the Rainbow Division. He retired from the Army in 1937. When the US entered World War II, General MacArthur was recalled to active duty and conducted a brilliant but unsuccessful defense of the Philippines, for which he was awarded the Medal of Honor. His citation reads: "For conspicuous leadership in preparing the Philippine Islands to resist conquest, for gallantry and intrepidity above and beyond the call of duty in action against invading Japanese forces, and for the heroic conduct of defensive and offensive operations on the Bataan Peninsula. He mobilized, trained, and led an army which has received world acclaim for its gallant defense against a tremendous superiority of enemy forces in men and arms. His utter disregard of personal danger under heavy fire and aerial bombardment, his calm judgment in each crisis, inspired his troops, galvanized the spirit of resistance of the Filipino people, and confirmed the faith of the American people in their Armed Forces."

Perhaps the most controversial time of his life was when President Truman fired him in April, 1951, for reasons that are still debated today. Upon his return to the U.S., MacArthur was given a ticker-tape parade in New York City. His final address to the graduating class at West Point (January 1962) is considered one of his finest speeches: We fight a war to win, not to appease the enemy.

MacArthur Park (originally Westlake Park) is a park in the Westlake neighborhood of Los Angeles. In the early 1940s, it was renamed after General Douglas MacArthur.

In 1967, producer Bones Howe asked songwriter Jimmy Webb to create a pop song with classical elements, different movements, and changing time signatures for a singing group called The Association and delivered "MacArthur Park" to Howe, but Howe did not care for the ambitious arrangement or unorthodox lyrics. The song was rejected by the group. Richard Harris was the first to record it in 1968.

Macbeth (*Mac Beatha* means "son of life" in Gaelic.)

Shakespeare's Macbeth killed the elderly Duncan in his sleep, which was not historically accurate. In the illustration below, we see a woman named Gruach MacDuff (daughter of Boite mac Cenaeda, and granddaughter of Kenneth II or III) standing between Duncan and Macbeth. Perhaps she was the real "Lady Macbeth."

Macbeth's father was King Finlay mac Ruaidri of Moray. Not long before Gruach got married to Macbeth's cousin Gillacomgain (in 1030), her fiancé and his brother (Malcolm, Mormaer of Moray) murdered King Finlay and placed their own father on the throne. Macbeth fled, most likely to Ireland. The birth of Gruach's son Lulach gave the Morays a potential future claimant to the Scottish throne.

In 1030, Macbeth returned to Moray to kill Gillacomgain during a *Game of Thrones*-type feast (burning him alive in a hall with fifty men). Shortly afterwards, he married his cousin's widow Gruach. Macbeth became step-father of Lulach and raised him as his own heir. Not long after Macbeth's return, Gruach's brother was murdered (1033), probably by Malcolm II, in order to clear the way for Duncan's inheritance.

In 1034, Duncan was crowned King of Scotland, five days after Malcolm II's death. He was not murdered by Macbeth while a guest in his castle, as Shakespeare's story goes. Instead, Duncan marched into Moray with an army in 1040 AD. Macbeth killed Duncan himself.

Macbeth and Gruach did not have any children of their own, but Gruach's son Lulach become heir to both crowns of Moray and Scotland. In 1050, Macbeth and Gruach took a pilgrimage to Rome, a trip that would have been unthinkable were they not secure on the throne.

Duncan's son Malcolm III returned from exile, causing Macbeth to abdicate the throne in Lulach's favour in 1057, but Lulach was killed by Malcolm in March, 1058. Lulach's son (Mael Snechtai, d. 1085) was at that time still a child, but Malcolm usurped the throne, removing Lulach's line from any hope of succession. The *Anglo-Saxon Chronicle* reported that

"*In this year* [1078] *Máel Coluim seized the mother of Máel Snechtai* [i.e., Gruach]... *and all his treasures, and his cattle; and he himself escaped [only] with difficulty.*"

The Weird Sisters

King James VI of Scotland (who became King James I of England) wrote a philosophical treatise on witchcraft and black magic. Published in 1597, it was called *Daemonologie*, and included subjects such as how demons bothered men, and also werewolves and vampires. It discussed the practices of sorcery, and the reasons that Christian society persecuted witches. The book was influential in revising judicial trial procedure involving witchcraft.

By the way, there is also a theory (one that holds water in my opinion) concerning Banquo, Thane of Lochaber. This theory holds that Banquo's son Fleance (who escaped Macbeth's murder spree) came to England *at the same time as* William the Conqueror (however, there is no record of a knight named Fleance coming *with* him). Fleance had a son named Walter, who had a son named Alan, Thane of Lochaber. Thus, Walter FitzAlan, 1st High Steward of Scotland, was not the son of Alan FitzFlaald, of the line of the Seneschals of Dol, as commonly believed, but rather, the great-great grandson of Banquo. Walter's mother was Adelina of Oswestry, daughter of Alan FitzFlaald, making Walter his *grand*son.

Macbeth Engraving, 1750

Shakespeare's Weird Sisters

McCall

The McCall family was among the ancient Dalriadan clans. Their name comes from the Gaelic *Mac Gall*, which means *son of the battle chief,* or Saint Gall (ca. 550-646), originally named Cellach or Caillech, Saint Gall was abbot and the apostle of the Suevi and the Alemanni, and might have been an Irishman of noble lineage, of the sept of Hy-Cennsealach, his mother being a queen of Hungary.

When Columbanus, Gall and Magnus left Ireland for mainland Europe, they took with them learning and the written word. The books were painstakingly reproduced on vellum by monks across Europe. Many of the Irish texts destroyed in Ireland during Viking raids were preserved in Abbeys across the channel

One evening as Gall was travelling in the woods of what is now Switzerland, he was warming his hands by a fire. A bear emerged from the woods and charged. Saint Gall rebuked the bear – it was so awed by his presence that it stopped its attack and slinked off toward the trees. There it gathered firewood before returning to share the heat of the fire with Saint Gall. The legend says that for the rest of his days Gall's companion the bear followed him around.

McCall's Magazine dates back to 1873, when a Scottish immigrant named James McCall created a publication called *The Queen: Illustrating McCall's Bazaar Glove-Fitting Patterns* as a vehicle for marketing his dressmaking patterns. After James McCall died in 1884, his widow continued the magazine with George Bladworth. At first they renamed it *The Queen of Fashion*, then in 1897, they called it *McCall's Magazine*.

St. Gall and the Bear

McCall's Magazine, 1907

McCarthy

The name McCarthy in Gaelic means *Mac Carthaigh*, from the word "carthach," which means "loving." Saint Carthach the Elder (d. ca. 580), was the brother of St. Cuanna and the great-grandson of Naill of the Nine Hostages, who died about the year 405.

McCarthyism is a name given to the period in American history (the 1950s) when U.S. Sen. Joseph McCarthy of Wisconsin led a series of investigations and hearings in an effort to expose communist infiltration into various areas of the U.S. government.

Actors blacklisted during the McCarthy era included Charlie Chaplin, Orson Welles, Burgess Meredith, Lena Horne, Langston Hughes, Arthur Miller, Pete Seeger, Gypsy Rose Lee, Leonard Bernstein, Dorothy Parker, John Garfield, Burl Ives, Judy Holliday, Uta Hagen, Artie Shaw, Dashiell Hammett and Lloyd Bridges. (I wonder who would be blacklisted today?)

When I first went to college in 1966, there were some people (probably not students) who said they belonged to a group called "Students for a Democratic Society" (SDS). That was simply a euphemism for Communism. One guy sat down with me and asked, "Do you believe in values?" What? I asked him what "values" were, and he went on about this and that and the other thing. Well, if you don't have values, I guess that just makes you a vegetable, which I guess is what he was trying to do to me, so I never spoke with any of them again. (In fact, I lampooned them in my novel *The Lyre Birds*, calling them "Junior Dolphins.")

I heard that this movement "progressed" until the 1990s, when students (or agitators) at colleges throughout the country insisted on their colleagues following rules of "Political Correctness" (PC). This was ostensibly to prevent them from accidentally hurting the feelings of the poor minorities. However, they were so aggressive about it that it began to stifle any possibility of meaningful dialogues about various subjects. In my opinion, "political correctness" is an oxymoron, that is, a phrase which contradicts itself. "Political" refers to having a reasonable debate about an issue, with both sides having a voice. "Correctness" implies that there is only one possible position… "mine."

Today (2022) I hear that the situation in American universities has reached the point of being intolerable (a perfect adjective, in this context). Take the example of Yeonmi Park, a girl who escaped North Korea with her mother, was enslaved in Mongolia, escaped to South Korea, and then moved to America. She describes Columbia University as "worse than North Korea" in terms of [lack of] freedom of speech.

McCain (Gaelic meaning "Son of Cahan" – see Agnes O'Cahan, Table 9)

As a youth, I had not been very politically oriented. I looked on in amusement as my college roommates campaigned for George McGovern; they were devastated by his loss to Richard Nixon. How could they be so personally involved in who was president? Later when B'Lack O'Bama (half Irish?) inched out Sen. John McCain I, too, felt a sense of despair, yet also a sense of dismay at how many Americans could have been duped by that guy's golf-ball-in-the-cheeks speech.

There had been a news article explaining that as a whole, on a scale of 1-100 (one being far left, one hundred being far right), Americans averaged 53. O'Bama stood at 43, ten points to the left of average; McCain stood at 56, three points to the right of average. With that in mind, I figured that I personally stood right up there with McCain at 56, but owing to my family situation, that would go leftwards again, bringing me back to about 50.

For a detailed look at my political "manifesto," see the Essay on the Triumvirate at the end of this volume.

McCulloch (a name of Celtic origin, possibly *MacCullaich,* translated as "son of a boar")

Benjamin McCulloch (1811-1862) was a soldier in the Texas Revolution, a Texas Ranger, and a Brigadier General of the Confederate Army during the Civil War. He was a descendant of Nicolas Martiau, a French Huguenot settler of Jamestown, Virginia. His family moved from North Carolina to Tennessee, where Davy Crockett had a great influence on young Ben. Ben went to St. Louis, but he was too late to join an expedition of fur trappers.

In 1835 Davy Crocket went to Texas, and Ben, tired of farming and seeking adventure, went with him. Ben came down with the measles, which prevented him from joining the massacre at the Alamo. At the Battle of San Jacinto in 1836, he commanded "Elizabeth" one of the "Twin Sisters" (the other cannon being named "Eleanor"), in honor of Crockett's widow Elizabeth.

He later joined the Texas Rangers, where he became known as an Indian fighter. He was elected to the Texas House of Representatives, but got into a rifle duel with Col. Reuben Ross, which left his right arm crippled for life. (His brother Henry later killed Ross with a pistol.)

In the Civil War, at the Battle of Pea Ridge (Arkansas), McCulloch, wearing a civilian black velvet suit and Wellington boots (he had a distaste for army uniforms), was shot off his horse by sharpshooter Peter Pelican. He did instantly. Brig. Gen. James McIntosh, second in command, was also killed trying to recover McCulloch's body.

McCulloch County, Texas, was formed in 1856 and named after him.

McCartney (Gaelic *Mac Cartaine*, diminutive of "Art")

James Paul McCartney was the son of James (and Mary Mohin), son of Joseph (a tobacco cutter, and Florence Clegg), son of James (a plumber and painter, and Elizabeth Williams), son of James (born in Ireland in 1820). Paul's great-grandfather James McCartney the Plumber moved from Ireland to Galloway, Scotland, probably during the Great Famine of 1845-1852. From there he moved to Liverpool.

In 1957, Paul McCartney joined John Lennon, another resident of Liverpool, who had formed a rock band called the Quarrymen. In 1960, they changed their name to the Beatles. By the time the Beatles hit the American scene, I was a freshman in high school. We had been raised on that sleepy, schmaltzy pop music that you hear regurgitated in movies like Grease and TV shows like Glee. It was your standard three-chord rock: C, F and G, fast, slow, and anywhere in between. Then the Beatles came along with their German haircuts, their Nehru jackets, their strangely fresh harmonies, and their eight-armed drummer (Richard Starkey, a.k.a. Ringo Starr).

The Beatles were to music as $i + 1$ [Stephen Krashen's term] is to foreign language learning. What I mean is, the status quo was always being rattled by something radically different, and that new something eventually became the status quo, until another radically different something came along and shattered the new status quo, and on and on. Each time B. Mitchell Reed, my favorite announcer on KFWB (who, by the way, was personally responsible for introducing the Beatles to the Ed Sullivan Show in 1962) would say, "And that was the newest release by the Beatles."

My friend and I wanted to see what all the fuss was about (we were fans of the Rolling Stones), so we went to Dodger Stadium to see the Beatles. We could hardly hear for all the screaming, but I must say, it was a memorable experience. In the end, though, it was only rock 'n' roll.

Enter George Martin, composer, arranger, producer. Thanks to George Martin, the Beatles emerged from their black and white cocoon in Living Color. He orchestrated their music, gave it a classical touch, breathed magic into it.

Even without the magic of George Martin, Paul McCartney's music gradually left the confines of three-chord rock and turned into something remarkable. McCartney's style is often characterized as optimistic, wistful, and harmonious. His songs cover an eclectic range of styles. McCartney was psychologically less introspective, more exuberant, and less focused on his own distress than his band-mate John Lennon.

Father McKenzie, a name used in the song "Eleanor Rigby" (*Revolver* album, 1966), was simply taken from a telephone directory. "Father McKenzie writing the words to a sermon that no one will hear…"

McKenzie (The Gaelic form of the name is *Mac Coinnich* or *Mac Choinnich,* meaning *son of Coinneach.*)

Scott McKenzie (born Philip Wallach Blondheim III) changed his name to Scott (because people said he looked like a Scottie dog, but he didn't like being called "Scottie"), and McKenzie (after his friend John Phillips' daughter MacKenzie Phillips).

Father McKenzie (see McCartney, above). This is a fictional character who appears in the song "Eleanor Rigby" by the Beatles: "Father McKenzie, wiping the dirt from his hands as he walks from the grave…"

McGregor (The Gaelic form of the name was *Mac Griogain,* which translates as son of *Gregory.*)

The McGregors' origins can be traced back to Griogair, son of the 8th century King Alpin of Scotland, the High King of the Scots and Picts.

Ewan McGregor was born in Perth, Scotland. His mother was Carol Diane Lawson, and his father was James Charles Stewart McGregor. Between 1999 and 2005 he played Obi-Wan Kenobi in the Star Wars Trilogy.

Unrelated to Ewan, MacGregor Sports Equipment is based in Albany, Georgia. They specialize in golf clubs, bags, and accessories. The company began in 1829 when Archibald and Ziba Crawford began manufacturing shoes. John McGregor joined the company in 1874, and the company changed from making footwear to making golf clubs, which at the time were made of wood. The company was acquired by Goldsmith during the 1930s, but they liked the name MacGregor (with slightly different spelling) better than Goldsmith, so they kept that name.

MacLean (Gaelic *Mac Gille Eathain,* son of a servant of St. John)

This author remembers distinctly the gracious act of the MacLean brothers, possibly named Don and James, who stopped their car in front of my father's house in the Vineyard in a Cove every Christmas Eve and played carols on their trumpets. Does that kind of America still exist somewhere? If so, kindly let me know where. I would love to go there.

McIntosh (from the Gaelic name *Mac an Toisich*, which means "son of the chief, or thane.")

Members of this distinguished Pictish family were said to have descended from Seach MacDuff, who was appointed Constable of Inverness Castle for his support of King Malcolm IV in Moray in 1160. A son of Seach then assumed the name "Mac-an-Toisch" and thus began the Clan MacIntosh.

In 1946, Frank McIntosh, helped design a high power, low distortion tube-type amplifier. This amplifier would later become the 50W-1.

McIntosh amplifiers were used at the Woodstock Music Festival in 1969. The Grateful Dead's "Wall of Sound" reputedly used forty-eight 300-watt per channel McIntosh solid state amplifiers for a total of 28,800 watts of continuous power.

MacDuff (The Gaelic form of the name is *Mac Dhuibh*.)

The historical Duff was a 10th century King of Alba, whose reign suffered from pervasive witchcraft. However, their clan remained the most powerful family in Fife during the Middle Ages.

In Shakespeare's play (*Macbeth*, ca. 1606), the contrast between Macduff and Macbeth is evidenced by their approaches to death. Macduff, reacts with a tortured grief to news of his family's death. He regards a capacity for emotional sensitivity to be the mark of a man. By contrast, Macbeth and Lady Macbeth insist that manhood implies a denial of feeling.

McLaren (The Gaelic form of the name is *Mac Labhruinn,* which means *son of Labhran* or *son of Laurence.*)

The Clan is believed to be descended from Lorn, son of Erc, who landed in Argyll in 503 AD (see #89-90 above). The surname McLaren was first found in Argyllshire, the region of western Scotland corresponding roughly with the ancient Kingdom of Dál Riata, in the Strathclyde region. They always remained faithful to the Royal House of Stewart.

Bruce McLaren (1937-1970) was a New Zealand race-car designer, driver, engineer and inventor, namesake of the Team McLaren race car team. In 1963, he created Bruce McLaren Motor Racing as a way of developing and racing sports cars. In the 1990s his successors began to use carbon fiber in racecars, which had never been used for racing cars before but was commonly used in aerospace. From there, the success of McLaren continued.

McMillan (Gaelic *Mac Mhaolain*, son of a bald man) The name McMillan may refer to a member of a religious order.

In 1877 John Thomas Stewart (1854-1937) married Louisa Ophelia McMillan (1861-1895), daughter of Wm Hugh McMillan and Lucinda Chandler. They had seven children: Cora Lee ('77), David Abney ('79), Charles Madison ('81), Harvey Hugh ('84), Margaret Elsie ('86), Alva Clinton ('89), and Atlee Draper ('92).

David Abney Stewart wrote a book called *Texas Poems, by a Texan*. I probably met him once when I was a child. It was after a Christadelphian Church meeting in Pomona, where they served real wine for Communion (my parents wouldn't let me drink it). I definitely remember Uncle Harvey being there afterwards, but he wouldn't remember me, as children are meant to be seen and not heard; Uncle Harvey was blind. I asked my father what happened, but in his typical minimalistic communication style, he simply answered, "Self-inflicted gunshot wound, which only severed the optical nerve." This is a poem written by John Thomas Stewart, Louisa Ophelia McMillan's husband, after she died in 1895. It is called "Despondency."

> Disappointment and failures my spirit has wounded
> And age my ambition has curbed.
> The summit of life is now reached and I look
> For the future to bring no reward.
>
> Gloom hovers around me like clouds in a storm.
> The tempest breaks loud on my ear
> Its thunders are pealing, but never a word
> Of comfort and peace can I hear.
>
> The things that I promised myself in my youth,
> Oh, where are they now, I would ask?
> They are gone never more to return I'm afraid,
> So life's without comfort at last.
>
> Foreboding so drear, Oh cease me to haunt
> Give rest to my spirit, I pray,
> Let the sun once more shine and brighten my path,
> Before I shall close up my day.
>
> If no respite I have, no relief from my cares,
> Oh how can this burden be borne?
> If these shadows continue my life to enshroud,
> Then away with my hopes so forlorn.
>
> As the slave to his cabin goes, weary and worn,
> When the day of his toil has been passed
> So I shall lie down at the end of my time
> And be conquered by death at the last.

McWherter (The name McWherter denotes "MacChruiters, Son of the Harper." Chruit, cithar, crwth, guitar, all refer to a stringed instrument.)

    Motto: *Te Deum laudamus*   Motto Translation: We praise thee, O God.

In 1346, King David II of Scotland granted a charter of the land of Dalelachane, in the earldom of Carrick to Patrick, son of Michael, harper of Carrick.

Many clans left Scotland because of religious persecution, usually by Catholics against Protestants. In the 1550s, groups called Covenanters began to form, bound by oath to the Presbyterian religion. In 1679, many of the McWhirter families that lived in the southwest of Scotland faced a period of deadly persecution. One John McWhirter died at sea off the coast of Orkney, while being captured as a rebel and condemned as a slave to be sent to the North American plantations. A large number of the McWhirter families in the southwest of Scotland migrated to the Ulster Plantation in the north of Ireland at the beginning of the seventeenth century.

Hugh McWhorter (1670-1759) was a successful linen merchant by trade. In 1729 Hugh, along with his wife and children, emigrated to the American colonies. At that time the Penn family of Pennsylvania and Delaware were recruiting Irish settlers to the American frontier in an effort to displace the Indians and to discourage other colonists from coming from Maryland, a Catholic colony. Hugh settled his family on farmland in Pencader Hundred, New Castle County, where he remained, a successful farmer, until his death.

Alexander McWhorter, one of Hugh's sons, went to North Carolina after his father's death, but returned to attend the College of New Jersey (now Princeton University). He served as a trustee of Princeton from 1772 until 1807.

In my early teens I met Ray of the McWherter clan. He made a gallant attempt to be a "big brother" to me. He wrote car songs with me ("Barracuda," "Volkswagen"); he took me on sports car rallies, that is, "obstacle" courses, in which you picked up a token at designated check-points along the route; he even took me to the Nexus club in Santa Barbara, a folk-singing club, which didn't really fit in with his persona, but he figured it fit in with mine, so there we went.

Other famous McWh*rters (a commonly used symbol indicating the various spellings of the name, using -e-, -i-, or -o-) were Ross & Norris McWhirter (twins) – who published the *Guinness Book of Records*, and James Harper – Publisher of Harper (and Rowe).

Some Fictional Mc's

Cecil McBee. The real-life Cecil McBee is an American jazz musician (he plays string bass). In the 1960s he moved from Oklahoma to New York, where his career as a studio musician took off. He currently teaches at the New England Conservatory in Boston.

In the 2000s, McBee unsuccessfully sued a Japanese clothing retailer that used his name for their chain stores.

Charlie McCarthy. Edgar Bergen (1930-1979) started his ventriloquist act in high school. His laptop dummy, Charlie McCarthy, was a wisecracking, misbehaving and flirtatious kid, dressed in a tuxedo, top hat, and wearing a monocle. They debuted on NBC's "Royal Gelatin Hour" in 1936 and had popular appearances on TV and in movies (with co-star Mortimer Snerd) until 1977.

Scrooge McDuck. Created in 1947 by Carl Barks, Donald Duck's Uncle Scrooge, speaking with a Scottish accent, quickly became one of the most popular Disney characters. Named after Ebenezer Scrooge, the fictional Scrooge lives in Duckburg, in the fictional state of Calisota. His famous "Money Bin" is filled with the wealth that he has accumulated through miserliness.

Marty McFly. Martin Seamus McFly, played by Michael J. Fox, is the protagonist of the film series *Back to the Future*. His family is supposedly of Irish descent. The original time frame is 1985, but when Marty meets Dr. Emmett "Doc" Brown with his famous DeLorean gull-winged car, he travels back to 1955, where he inspires Chuck Berry to play raspy rock songs on his guitar.

Mrs. McGillicuddy. On the "I Love Lucy" show (1951-1957) Mrs. McGillicuddy, played by Kathryn Card, is Lucy's scatterbrained mother. She causes Lucy's husband Ricky Ricardo all kinds of trouble, attempting to go on a trip to California (they lived in New York) with them and their neighbors Fred and Ethel. She also sent Tennessee Ernie Ford to stay with them without telling Ricky that it was an important chance for his band to play at the Roxy.

Mr. Magoo. Jim Backus (1913-1989) was the voice-over actor of this popular cartoon character, beginning in 1949. J. Quincy Magoo was a little old rich guy, famously near-sighted, who always got into comical situations, but got out of them through his uncanny streaks of luck. His butler was named Worcestershire.

Essay
The Triumvirate, or,
The Laws of Nova Dalriada

This is a fanciful description of the perfect state, named after that ancient kingdom that straddled the Irish Channel, including parts of Northern Ireland and Western Scotland. (The name *Nova Scotia*, or New Scotland, was already taken, being a province of Canada; that is why I chose the name of an older kingdom.)

NAME OF COUNTRY: Nova Dalriada

GOVERNMENT STRUCTURE

The government should consist of an Executive branch, a Legislative Branch, and a Judicial Branch. The Legislative Branch should make laws. The Judicial Branch should judge whether the laws are just. The Executive Branch should enforce the laws.

EXECUTIVE BRANCH

The Executive Branch shall consist of a Triumvirate, that is, three leaders whom I have called "Mice," after a children's book called *City Mouse, Country Mouse*, by Maggie Rudy.

City Mouse (elected by city-dwellers) - responsible for economic issues;
Country Mouse (elected by counties) - responsible for food, water, land, etc.;
Global Mouse (a king, chosen by single combat) - responsible for foreign relations.

"Single combat" may comprise any method that is mutually agreed upon by
all concerned parties, for example, a push-up contest, an arm-wrestling bout,
or even Russian roulette, as long as it has some test of physical courage
and a clear indication of victory.

Terms may be staggered, for example, three-, four-, or five years.

This functions somewhat like those countries like Finland that have both
a president and a prime minister: one for domestic affairs, one for foreign affairs.

LEGISLATIVE BRANCH

Based on observed facts, some people are predisposed to making money independently; others are good at working, but not independently; still others are not good at working and are prone to social dependance.*

Accordingly, a representative government should have three "houses," or national assemblies: a House of Benevolence, a House of Fellows, and a House of Wards. These would create laws by voting amongst themselves, to wit: laws governing the interaction of citizens with the law itself, taxation, property, land and houses, commerce, family matters and inheritance, physical assault, non-physical assault, agriculture, labor issues, welfare.**

If two of the three houses agree, they may send a proposal to the three executive "mice." Again, if two of the three agree, they would sign it into law. If not, they would return the proposal to the houses, which may vote by a super-majority to overturn the veto.***

The filibuster is an ingenious device designed to protect the nation against a simple 51-49 majority, in which 49% of the people are likely to suffer unjust laws. Since the filibuster requires a 60% passing rate, there must be compromise, which has long-term benefits for all.

As with the Executive Branch three-, four-, or five-year staggered terms may serve to distribute responsibility evenly.

* These three classes of people are explicitly referred to in the *Code of Hammurabi* as Gentlemen, Commoners and Slaves. Though modern society despises such terminology, we tacitly acknowledge this fact of human predisposition.

** I originally thought these three houses should read "Benevolence, Fellowship, Dependency," but these might have different connotations among different groups. "Fellows" reminds us of the incorporated member of a college, indicating acceptance, possibility. For those who argue that the third group may be incapable of governing themselves, let me answer your objection. Wards (Dependents) would include all those persons receiving some form of government assistance, that is, welfare payments, disability, as well as a large group of elderly persons receiving government pensions. These would come from all walks of life and would be perfectly capable of participating in meaningful representative government.

*** Failures such as Britain's weakened House of Lords (Parliament Act of 1911; Salisbury Convention, 1945) should be avoided. Similarly, the American failure in the 17th Amendment, which led to a popular vote for senators, not to mention opening both houses to members of all three classes, should be avoided.

JUDICIAL BRANCH

Which brings us to the Court of Last Resort. I personally see no problem whatsoever with the American system of weighing laws through the courts, one after another, until finally they are decided (in some cases) by a supreme court. The main problem, as seen by some, is the method of nomination of its justices, and their tenure. This could be solved by the Triumvirate, in which the three "mice" appoint justices, whose term may be limited by an agreed-upon number of years.

MONEY

The monetary unit shall be the price of one hamburger. No lettuce, no pickles.*
1 Burger = 99 Fries (3 x 33, or three Ounces). This is an inflation-proof standard.
Therefore the monetary units are: 1 Burger = 3 Ounces; 1 Ounce = 33 Fries.**

---

* Adam Smith, in *The Wealth of Nations*, claims that adhering to a gold standard will always put a nation at risk of losing its wealth due to a foreign invasion. It is unlikely that any invasion could successfully steal all a country's hamburgers (not impossible... just unlikely).

** One McDonald's hamburger equals 3 ounces. (A quarter-pounder equals 4 ounces.) A package of McDonald's fries includes: Large = 100 pieces, Medium = 68 pieces, Small = 58 pieces. If we go back to the earth : moon ratio (11:3), eleven in Spanish is "once." We may multiply three *times* eleven to get an Ounce or 33 Fries, and three times a "thrice" to get 99 Fries, or a Burger.

ENFRANCHISEMENT

Voting Rights: Single men or women - 1 Vote, Married - 2 matching votes for one pair.
In order to preserve the unity of household, a husband may have two matching votes, (so the husband and wife do not cancel each other's votes).
Eligibility - over 21, based on an ever-evolving civics / history / economics test.

While many may see this as a revocation of women's rights, it may be offset by creating a tax system in which a married couple pays 2/3 as much tax as single men or women.

Other Electoral Rules

If the nation is so large as to have several time zones, elections shall be held during a single twenty-four hour period, based on the time at the Capital. This is to prevent news outlets from "calling" the results of an election, based on results of polls closed in the east, possibly influencing voters in the west, where polls are still open.

No absentee ballots, mail-in ballots, early or late ballots shall be allowed. All voting must be done in person, during the twenty-four hour voting period.

No local issues shall be placed on ballots pertaining to the national election. This will reduce time spent at the polling station, eliminating the need for voters to decide on issues such as local school board members, or who shall be in charge of tending the trees lining city sidewalks.

Practices such as the Electoral College make good sense, in that they provide a buffer against the popular vote, which may be corrupted by lack of education, influence groups, social stigmas, etc.

LAND OWNERSHIP

The nation shall be divided into ten regions; each region shall have nine states; each state shall have eight zones; each zone shall have seven counties, according to their geographical layouts.

A township of 5,040 residents or more shall be divided into eight neighborhoods, each neighborhood having seven watchmen.

Should a city have more than 50,400 residents, it shall have nine precincts, each with eight neighborhoods, with seven watchmen for each neighborhood.*

If there should arise a city, either congruent with its county, or within its boundaries, that city shall be divided into ten boroughs; each borough shall have nine precincts; each precinct eight 'hoods; each 'hood shall have seven watchmen.

* Plato liked the number 5040 for its pure mathematical qualities ($10 \times 9 \times 8 \times 7 = 5040$).

- 5040 has exactly 60 divisors, counting itself and 1.
- 5040 is the largest factorial ($7! = 5040$) that is also a highly composite number.
- 5040 is the sum of 42 consecutive primes (23 + 29 + 31 + 37 + 41 + 43 + 47 + 53 + 59 + 61 + 67 + 71 + 73 + 79 + 83 + 89 + 97 + 101 + 103 + 107 + 109 + 113 + 127 + 131 + 137 + 139 + 149 + 151 + 157 +163 + 167 + 173 + 179 + 181 + 191 + 193 + 197 + 199 + 211 + 223 + 227 + 229).

As of 2018, there were 19,495 incorporated cities, towns and villages in the United States. 14,768 of these had populations below 5,000. 4,727 had populations over 5000.

As the moon circles the earth to protect her, 3:11 of the area of the nation, excluding waterways, which are in the public domain, shall be owned by the Crown; that is, a portion equal to 1080 of each 5040 counties. Of each fourteen residences, the three owned by the Crown shall be used for housing public wards. At least seven shall be privately owned. No more than four shall be rented to tenants. All rental units must be owned by individuals or small companies, none by large corporations.

Furthermore, the price of rents should be no more than one-fourth of a family's monthly income, (assuming that both husband and wife are working full-time), or a pro-rated figure based on the number of square feet of the lodging (see table below), whichever is more.

Size (in square feet)	Income (in Burgers)	x 1/4 = Rent	Burgers per Sq Ft
Studio 225 sq ft	1,000 B / mo	250 B	1.0 B / sq ft
	2,000 B / mo	500 B	2.0 B / sq ft
1 Bdrm 450 sq ft	3,000 B / mo	750 B	1.5 B / sq ft
	4,000 B / mo	1,000 B	2.0 B / sq ft
	5,000 B / mo	1,250 B	2.5 B / sq ft
2 Bdrm 675 sq ft	6,000 B / mo	1,500 B	2.0 B / sq ft
	7,000 B / mo	1,750 B	2.4 B / sq ft
	8,000 B / mo	2,000 B	2.8 B / sq ft
3 Bdrm 900 sq ft	9,000 B / mo	2,250 B	2.5 B / sq ft
	10,000 B / mo	2,500 B	2.7 B / sq ft

MARRIAGE AND THE FAMILY

Marriage is defined as the physical, legal and moral bond between one man and one woman. A man is defined biologically as a person with both x and y chromosomes; a woman is defined biologically as a person with two x chromosomes. The purpose of marriage is to glorify God, to provide companionship, and to produce offspring.

Issues

Certain issues such as Willful Termination of Pregnancy (hereafter referred to as Wil-Ter-Pre, or WilTerPre-tation) need to be resolved. As a child, I regarded Wilterpretation as something a whore did with a coat hanger. Nowadays some people see it as something respectable women do with a clinician. Declining moral standards; improving sanitary conditions.

Whatever your moral position, there are three people whose opinions count: the father, the mother, and the baby. Since the baby cannot voice its opinion, the state should step in to be its advocate. The people's representatives at the local level should establish laws that pertain to the willful termination of pregnancy. The other two concerned voices would be that of the mother and that of the father. Two of the three voices (including the unborn's representative) should agree before terminating a pregnancy. If the father cannot be found, a proxy should be appointed by a court.

In any event, since Wilterpretation results in the death of a person, an appropriate consequence should be established, whether penitentiary, monetary, or meaningful community service. It would be up to the local representative legislature to decide who should pay the consequences, whether the father, the mother, or a designated proxy, such as an elected official or a relative.

Adoption would be a reasonable solution for mothers who could not raise their own children.*

---

* I grew up with friends who lived in the Masonic Home. No one ever disdained or disparaged them. Here are some SpaceBook posts about it:

Janine C: Hi , I am hoping you can help me. In 1959-1962 there was a home located on Covina Blvd., maybe a block away from Charter Oak high school. I had a friend who lived there in what might have been apartment / servants quarters over a garage I think… not in the main building. Possibly a bonus for good behavior. I cannot remember the name of it but I believe it was a home for kids (girls?) either wayward or otherwise. My friend would spend many weekends at our home. Her name was Jeanie. I have been searching for her for years without success. Do you by chance remember the name of the home? I believe the building is long gone now. My searches come up empty. Thank you.

HouseParents: I am sure that was the Masonic Children's Home. Are you related to Wayne and Dennis Cox?

(*FN continued on following page)

Other issues would include twisting the definition of marriage partners to include persons other than heterosexual pairs. While this might serve the purpose of providing companionship (will it one day be extended to marrying pets, or trees, or even favorite authors?), it fails to glorify God, and it cannot possibly satisfy the purpose of producing offspring. Perhaps if some governments wish to make provisions for old maids or confirmed bachelors to share accommodations for companion-ship, it would be considered, but provisions should involve *rights* for individuals, not *benefits*.

If I may take a term which is in vogue today and apply it to education, the acronym LGBTQ should mean Let's Get Better Teachers Quickly.

EDUCATION

Education is the process of passing down, or encouraging the acquisition of, knowledge, skills, values, morals, beliefs, habits, and personal development. The values of good citizenship include community, affirmation, productivity, responsibility, restoration and integrity.

The national core curriculum should be based on these subjects: mother tongue and literature, foreign languages, mathematics, environmental studies, biology, geography, physics, chemistry, health education, religion, ethics, history, social studies, music, visual arts, crafts, physical education, home economics (Finland, 2022).

Public universities should have a balance of political representation among faculty that reflects that of the local population. Private universities that receive federal funding shall balance their political representation against that proportion of their total budget. Student loans shall be allotted for majors in proportion to provable job opportunities in those fields.

* My Reply (continued from page 143): No, the Home was located down there near the entrance to the Mesa, across from Badillo School. That place you're talking about was more like a mental institution. I lived on Cypress Avenue, one block away from Covina Blvd, and also a block away from Charter Oak H.S. One day I was playing in our front yard when I saw a girl lurking in the bushes [wearing a night-gown]. I asked if she was my sister's friend, but she didn't answer. Then two guys wearing white coats came up and grabbed her off.
  Wayne Cox and I were lab assistants in the chemistry class. One day we poured sulfur down the drain, causing the whole wing to be evacuated. He probably moved to Seattle to get away from people like me.

POETRY

Why did Plato banish poets from his *Republic*? He banished them because they produced the wrong sort of poetry. Plato was concerned with finding truth. Since art imitates physical things, which in turn imitate absolute Forms, art is always a copy of a copy, in other words, an illusion. He believed poets distort truth by stirring the emotions, as did Homer. Plato argues that in Homer, gods are capricious, kings are spiteful, heroes are vengeful, and common soldiers are cowardly.

Sir Philip Sidney, though he probably would not have banned philosophers and historians from his Arcadia, believed that poetry combined the best aspects of philosophy and history. It inspires men towards virtuous acts, as does philosophy. It delights us, as does history (!).

Oddly, classical poetry imposed its own forms on subsequent generations. One poet who actually gained praise from future generations for refusing to submit to classical forms was Shakespeare, who totally disregarded the three unities of time, place, and action, as well as the unity of sentiment (that is, of not mixing the comic and the tragic).

Wordsworth and Coleridge, though in agreement that a waterfall could be described as "majestic," would have scoffed at the idea that it could have been described as both "sublime" and "beautiful," as the two words at that time (August 21, 1803, when they visited Cora Linn Falls) were perceived as mutually exclusive. Shelley espoused his own particular social and political agenda, cast in quasi-religious spiritual terms. In the context of doubt and decaying morals of the nineteenth century, Matthew Arnold totally transformed poetry into a surrogate for religion. T.S. Eliot, for his part, would probably have turned the *Republic* into a *Wasteland* by relegating poetry to the theater which, in the mid-twentieth century, provided a platform for a particular set of psycho-dramatists, excluding performances for entertainment (a role that was filled by the cinema).

Instead, poets should go back and reexamine Sir Philip Sidney's *Defence of Poetry*. Sidney outlines the different "parts" of poetry: heroic, lyric, tragic, comic, satiric, iambic, elegiac, and pastoral.

About heroic poetry Sidney writes, "Only let Æneas be worn in the tablet of your memory, how he governs himself in the ruin of his country; in the preserving his old father, and carrying away his religious ceremonies... how in storms, how in sports, how in war, how in peace, how a fugitive, how victorious, how besieged, how besieging, how to strangers, how to allies, how to enemies, how to his own; lastly, how in his inward self, and how in his outward government; and I think, in a mind most prejudiced with a prejudicating humor, he will be found in excellency fruitful..."

Do we have such heroes today? Would that the Nova Dalriada were filled with such people, and that its poets sang their praises.

Sidney concludes, "They [poets] cry out with an open mouth, as if they had overshot Robin Hood, that Plato banished them out of his Commonwealth. Truly this is much, if there be much truth in it."

In my opinion, the only poets that should be banned from Nova Dalriada are those whom I call "D-W-O" poets, that is, people whose oral readings sound like Death-Warmed-Over (D-W-O), as in Matthew Arnold's "reverent" world, so they must be read with a low, quiet, reverent voice.

Moreover, it is not the poets that should be banished from the Commonwealth, but rather the political lobbyists, as well as the PACs (political action committees). In a democracy, the people select representatives to carry their voices to the capital, to enact laws that serve the majority. In a system that permits lobbying, special interests with money can wine and dine those representatives, diluting or even negating the voices of the people. The same goes for PACs, which use money to run election campaigns. Both institutions run counter to the idea of pure Democracy.

The Song of Snorri and Skalli

If the Tower Ravens should cease their drawl,
    Fie fickle, foe fee,
    Caw cackle, and cree!
'Tis said the Commonwealth will fall.
    Fie fickle, foe fee,
    Caw cackle, and cree!
'Tis altogether fitting and proper*
    Fie fickle, foe fee,
    Caw cackle, and cree!
For Jan to be called the Big Bopper.
    Fie fickle, foe fee,
    Caw cackle, and cree!

If a quick brown fox jumps over the dog,
    Fie fickle, foe fee,
    Caw cackle, and cree!
A tadpole is known as a pollywog.
    Fie fickle, foe fee,
    Caw cackle, and cree!
If all good men come to their country's aid,
    Fie fickle, foe fee,
    Caw cackle, and cree!
Then I will pronounce all things done and said.
    Fie fickle, foe fee,
    Caw cackle, and cree!

* *Dulce et decorum est…*

WEIGHTS AND MEASURES

The problem with the so-called "metric" system is that different units of measure are based on different denominations of the "meter," which do not correspond to the basic unit. For example, the measure of length is the meter, or one ten-millionth of one quarter the circumference of the earth, taken from the North Pole to the Equator through Paris. This in turn is divided into smaller units using the Greek prefixes decimeter (1/10), centimeter (1/100), millimeter (1/1000), etcetera and into larger units using the Roman prefixes dekameter (x 10), hectometer (x 100), kilometer (x 1000), etc.

However the measure of volume is based on the liter, which is one thousand cubic centimeters, or one cubic decimeter (10cm x 10cm x 10cm).

As for mass, we begin with a gram, or the weight of one cubic centimeter of water (1/100m x 1/100m x 1/100m = 1/100,000,000m, or one cubic micrometer). The smaller unit is a milligram (1/1000), and the larger unit is a kilogram (1/10,000 x 1000 = 1/10m).

Furthermore, the General Conference on Weights and Measures met in Paris in 1960 and decreed that 1 meter should equal 1,650,763.73 wave lengths of krypton 86, a rare gas found in the atmosphere. Who goes around with a krypton yard stick to measure meters?

In a rational system, all units would be based on the basic unit, not on a denomination thereof. With this in mind, I propose an alternative standard of measure, which I call the Metric Cubit.*

Now if you wanted to continue to use the wavelength of krypton 86, we might be able to set up a reasonable Metric Cubit by establishing a length of 500,000 wavelengths, which would come out to about 30.289 cm. However, I prefer using the distance that light travels in one second. This is about 299,792,458 kilometers, and if we took 10^{-9} this distance, we would have a Metric Cubit (cu) equal to about 29.9792458 cm.

The square of this Metric Cubit (a square cubit, or cu^2) would equal 898.75 cm^2.

In volume, a cubiliter (cl) would equal 26,944 cm^3.

The equivalent mass (a cubigram, or cg) would equal 26.944 kg.

* Mathematicians John Taylor (1781–1864) and Sir John Herschel (1792-1871) sought to invent a new measuring unit to replace the existing British system. When Sir Isaac Newton (1642-1727) addressed the topic, he came up with the notion of a "Sacred Cubit," which measured 2.0736 English feet. Taylor recognized this as being 6/5 of an Egyptian cubit (1.728 English feet) and assumed that 6/5 was a "cubit-and-a-handsbreadth," as described in the Old Testament. He concluded that a cubit could be divided into 25 inches. After some sophisticated manipulation, Taylor suggested that the earth's polar radius should be divided into ten million "Sacred Cubits" of 25.0265 British inches each. However, there is another way to get there.

It seems that there were both shorter and longer versions of the Egyptian, Greek and Roman feet/cubits, but they were all related to one another. The proportion of longer to shorter units was 176:175. Here is an overview of their relations, including what I call an "Orphic" foot/cubit, which relates to the English measure.

$$1 \text{ Roman Foot/Cubit} \times 25/24 = 1 \text{ Greek Foot/Cubit}$$
$$1 \text{ Greek Foot/Cubit} \times 25/24 = 1 \text{ "Orphic" Foot/Cubit}$$
$$1 \text{ "Orphic" Foot/Cubit} \times 12/11 = 1 \text{ Egyptian Foot/Cubit}$$

Taylor made two critical mistakes in his calculations. The first occurred when he related Newton's "Sacred Cubit" with the longer Egyptian Cubit, but from there enlarged it by 176/175 to obtain a kind of "super-cubit." The second resulted from his assumption that Newton's cubit could be divided into five parts (after all, Henry VIII had already standardized the "hand," a measure for the height of horses—sometimes reckoned as four fingers plus a thumb—five of these "hands" would still be two inches longer than a cubit of eighteen inches, or three inches shorter than a "Sacred Cubit"). However, the ancient cubit was divided into *seven* handsbreadths of *four* fingers each. One additional handsbreadth would result in 8/7 of a cubit. The standard Old Testament cubit was therefore 8/7 times the *Greek* cubit rather than 6/5 times the *Egyptian* cubit. Hence there is no transmigration between shorter and longer units. The result is the Hebrew cubit equaling 1.73787425 English feet. Both calculations (Taylor's and Michell's) result in identical measurements for the earth's polar radius.

Both Taylor and Herschel possibly fell victim to the scientific trend of their time, a trend which I refer to as the Great Decimal Shift. They tended to seek out a system of measure which would lend itself to a base-ten system, as with the French metric system, instead of a base-twelve. In accordance with this trend, there would be exactly ten million "Sacred Cubits" of 25.0265 inches in the earth's polar radius (the measure taken by 8/7 Greek cubits would result in twelve million units in the polar radius). In short, there was really no need to "replace" the existing British system. It was already perfect, both in terms of measurement and in terms of pure number, that is, the powers of twelve:

Radius of Earth: $12^3 \times 2^4 / 7$ miles
Circumf. of Earth: $12^5 / 10$ miles
Circumf. of Moon: 12^7 feet

Ratio:	24:25	24:25		11:12		
	Roman	Greek	"Orphic"	Egyptian	"Sacred"	Hebrew
English Feet:						
175:	0.96768	1.008	1.05	1.1454545		
176:	0.9732096	1.01377	1.056	1.152		
Cubit:						
175:	1.45152	1.152	1.575	1.71818	x 8/7 Gr = 1.728	
176:	1.4598144	1.52064	1.584	1.728 x 6/5 Eg =	2.0736 x 8/7 Gr = 1.73787425 x 176/175 = 2.0854491	2.0854491

	x 5,000 ft =	x 5,000	x 5,000	x 5,000		
Mile:	4,866.048	5,068.8	5,280	5,760		

                                          2.0854491   1.73787425
                                          x 10 million   x 12 million
Polar Radius: 20,854,491 ft. 20,854,491 ft.

TIME

What is time, anyway? May I suggest that it is none other than life itself, for if we have life, we live in time; if things have no life, well…

Now our days are measured in 12-hour units. The problem is that as the earth travels around the sun, some days of the year are longer; some days are shorter. In the Nova Dalriada, each day should be 12 hours long, and each night should be 12 hours long. Here is the scheme:

Jan Feb Mar Apr May Jun Jul Aug Sep Oct Nov Dec

Jan Feb Mar Apr May Jun Jul Aug Sep Oct Nov Dec

As is shown in the illustration, the longest day of the year (in June) is represented by the widest distance between arcs of the curve; the shortest day (in December) is represented by the shortest distance. The length of the hours of day in summer shall be equal to the length of the hours of night in winter, and vice versa, for each day of the year.

SPORTS

This may strike some as a little weird, but bear with me. The visiting team in a game of baseball should run around the bases in a clockwise manner; the home team should run around the bases in a counter-clockwise manner. (After all, in games such as football and basketball, teams play in opposite directions.) The shortstop may stand wherever he feels it is most effective to stop the ball "short."

Games such as kickball (i.e., soccer) should be placed in the category of recreation, like dodgeball, and not sports.

Speaking of recreation, games such as skateboarding, ping-pong, and synchronized swimming should not be included in organized sporting competitions.

Appendix 1 – The Big Huge Bk of Mc

Number of Generations from Adam

Hebrews	Trojans / Scandinavians	Scythians / Milesians
1 Adam 4000-3070 BC	1 Adam 4000-3070 BC	1 Adam 4000-3070 BC
2 Seth	2 Seth	2 Seth
3 Enos	3 Enos	3 Enos
4 Cainan	4 Cainan	4 Cainan
5 Mahalaleel	5 Mahalaleel	5 Mahalaleel
6 Jared	6 Jared	6 Jared
7 Enoch	7 Enoch	7 Enoch
8 Methuselah	8 Methuselah	8 Methuselah
9 Lamech	9 Lamech	9 Lamech
10 Noah 2943-2007 BC	10 Noah 2943-2007 BC	10 Noah 2943-2007 BC
11 Shem	11 Shem	11 Japheth
12 Arphaxad Gen. 11:10-26	12 Arphaxad Gen. 11:10-26	12 Magog (+ Gomer)
13 Salah*	13 Salah*	13 Baoth, King of Scythia
14 Eber	14 Eber	14 Fenius Farsaidh, K. of Scythia
15 Peleg	15 Peleg	15 Niul Nemnach
16 Reu	16 Reu	16 Gaodhal Glas
17 Serug	17 Serug	17 Asruth
18 Nahor	18 Nahor	18 Sruth
19 Terah	19 Terah	19 Heber Scutt
20 Abram /Abraham 1992--1917	20 Abram /Abraham 1992--1917	20 Beouman
21 Isaac	21 Isaac	21 Oghaman, King of Scythia
22 Jacob	22 Jacob	22 Tait, King of Scythia
23 Judah b. 1752 BC Gen 29.35	23 Judah b. 1752 BC Gen 29.35	23 Agnan
24 Phares	24 Zarah	24 Lamhfionn Pr. of Scythia
25 Ezrom	25 Darda Dardaius	25 Eimhir Glunfionn 2213-
26 Aram	26 Erichthonius Illium K	26 Agnan Fionn 2180 –
27 Aminadab	27 Tros Acadia	27 Faobhar (Febric Glas) 2133
28 Naasson	28 Ilus Troy 1282 BC	28 Nenuall 1899-
29 Salmon	29 Laomedon Troy	29 Nuadhad 1880-
30 Boaz 1312 BC	30a Priam, High K. of Troy	30 Ealloid (Alladh) 1855-
31 Obed	30b Tithonus of Troy d. 1237 BC	31 Earchada (Arcadh) 1830-?
32 Jesse	31 Memnon Troy d. 1183 BC	32 Deaghata 1800- ?
	32 Tror (Thor)	

Hebrews	Trojans / Scandinavians	Scythians / Milesians
Kings of Israel / Judah:		
33 King David 1085-1015 BC	(The chronology does not line up	33 Brath
34 King Solomon d. 930	nicely here…	34 Breoghan 927-872
35 King Roboam 1002-913	…continued on next page.)	35 Bile 889-839
36 King Abia 970-911		36 Milesius 853-806 BC
37 King Asa 950-870		
38 King Josaphat 930-848		
39 King Joram 910-841		
40 King Ozias 893-841		
41 King Josiah 871-796		
42 King Amazaiah 849-767		
43 King Uzziah 812-739		
44 King Joatham 773-732		
45 King Achaz 753-716		
46 King Ezekias 741-687		
47 King Manasseh 709-642		
48 King Amon 664-640		
49 King Josiah 648-609		
50 Prince Johanan of Judah d. 609		
51 Tamar bat Johanan		
52 Tea Tephi		37 Heremon d. 1699 BC
54 Irial Faidh		38 K. Irial Faidh d. 1269 BC
55 Eithriall		39 K. Eithriall
56 Follain		40 Follain
57 Tighernmas		41 K. Tighernmas d. 1543 BC
58 Eanbotha		42 Eanbotha
59 Smiorguil		43 Smiorguil
60 Fiachadh Labhri		44 K. Fiachadh Labhri
61 Aongus Ollmuch		45 K. Aongus Ollmuch d. 1043 bc
62 Maoin		46 Maoin
63 Rotheachta		47 K. Rotheachta
64 Dein		48 Dein
65 Siorna Saoghalach		49 K. Siorna Saoghalach

Hebrews	Trojans / Scandinavians	Scythians / Milesians
66 Oliolla Olchaoin		50 Oliolla Olchaoin
67 K. Giallchadh		51 K. Giallchadh d. 787 BC
68 K. Nuadhas FionnFail		52 K. Nuahhas d. 745 BC
69 K. Aodhain Glas		53 K. Aodhain Glas
70 Simeon Breac		54 Simeon Breac
71 Muirteadach Bolgrach		55 Muirteadach Bolgrach
72 Fiachadh Toigrach		56 Fiachadh Toigrach
73 Duach Laidhrach		57 Duach Laidhrach
74 Eochaidh Bualgllerg		58 Eochaidh Bualgllerg
75 Ugaine More the Great		59 Ugaine More the Great
76 Cobhthach Coalbreag r. 591-451 BC		60 Cobhthach Coalbreag r. 591-451 BC
77 Meilage		61 Meilage
78 Jaran Gleofathach		62 K. Jaran Gleofathach
79 Coula Cruaidh Cealgach		63 K. Coula Cruaidh Cealgach
80 Oiliolla Caisfhiachach		64 K. Oiliolla Caisfhiachach
81 Eochaidh Foltleathan		65 K. Eochaidh Foltleathan
82 Aongns Tuirmheach (Teamharch 384-324 BC)	33 Loridi	66 K. Aongns Tuirmheach b. 384
	34 Einridi	67 K. Enda Aighneach b. 312 BC
83 Enda Aighneach r. 312-292 BC	35 Vingethor b. 210 BC	68 Labhra Suire
	36 Vingener	69 Blathucha
84 Labhra Suire	37 Moda	70 Easamhuin Famhua
85 Blathucha	38 Magi	71 Roighnein Ruadh
86 Easamhuin Famhua	39 Sceaf (Seskef)	72 Finlogha
87 Roighnein Ruadh	40 Bedwig b. 110 BC	73 Fian
88 Fionnlaoch	41 Hwala King of Goths	74 K. Eodchaidh Feidhlioch
89 Fian	42 Hathra (Athra)	75 Fineamhuas
90 Eochaidh Feidhlioch r. 142-130 BC	43 Itermon or Itormann	76 K. Lughaidh Raidhdearg
	44 Heremond	77 K. Criomhthan Niadhnar
91 Freas Nar-Lothar	45 Sceldwa de Troy	78 Fearaidhach Fion Feachtnuigh
92 Lughaidh Raidhdearg	46 Bedwa (Beaw), King of Troy	79 K. Fiachadh Fionoluidh
	47 Taetwa Tecti b. 55 AD	80 K. Tuathal Teachtmar b. 56 AD
		81 Felim

Hebrews	Trojans / Scandinavians	Scythians / Milesians
93 Criomhthan Niadhnar r. 7-9AD	48 Geata Jat Trojan	
94 Fearaidhach Feachtnuigh	49 Godwulf Trojan	
95 Fiachadh Fionoluidh	50 Flocwald of Asgard	
96 Tuathal Teachtmar b. 056 AD	51 Finn of Godwulf b. 130 AD	
97 Felim Rachtmar b. 80 AD	52 Frithuwulf	
98 K. Conn Ceadchathach	53 Frealaf	82 K. Conn Ceadchathach 100-B
(of 100 Battles)	54 Fredwulf, Frithuwald, or Bor	d. 157
99 Art Ean Flier	55 Odin b. 215 AD	83 K. Art Aonflier d. 195
100 Cormac Ulfada	56 Yngvi Tyrkja	84 K. Cormae Usada
101 Caibre Liffeachair d. 284 AD	57 Njord Odinsson K. of Swedes	85 K. Caibre Liffeachair d. 284
102 Fiachadh Sreabthuine	58 Yngvi Frey, King of Uppsala	86 K. Fiachadh Sreabthuine
103 Muireadhach Tireach	59 Fjolnir Yngvi Freysson	87 K. Muireadhach Tireach
104 Eochaidh Moigmeodhin	60 Svegdi Fjolnarsson	88 K. Eochaidh Moigmeodhin
105 Nail of the 9 Hostages d. 405	61 Vanlandi Svegdasson b. 298	89 K. Nail of the 9 Hostages
106 Eogan	62 Visbur Vanlandasson 319 AD	90 Eogan
107 Murireadhach	63 Domaldi Visbursson 340	91 K. Murireadhach
108 Erc	64 Domar Domaldasson 361	92 Erc
	65 Dyggvi I Domarsson 382	
Kings of Argyll:	66 Dag Dyggvasson 403	Kings of Argyll:
109 King Fergus More d. 501	67 Agni Dagsson 424	93 K. Fergus More d. 501
110 King Dongard	68 Alrek Agnasson	94 K. Dongard
111 King Conran	69 Yngvi Alreksson	95 K. Conran
112 King Aidan	70 Jorund Yngvasson	96 K. Aidan
113 King Eugene IV	71 Aun (The Aged) Ani 509	97 K. Eugene IV
114 King Donald IV	72 Egil Aunsson 530 AD	98 K. Donald IV
115 Dongard	73 Ottar (Vendilkraka) Egilsson	99 Dongard
116 King Eugene V	74 Adilis "Athils" Ottarsson	100 K. Eugene V
117 Findan	75 Eystein Adilsson 594	101 Findan
118 King Eugene VII	76 Yngvar Eysteinsson	102 K. Eugene VII
119 King Etfinus	77 Skira Ingvarsson 620	103 K. Etfinus
120 King Achaius	78 Radbard K. of Gardgarige	104 K. Achaius
121 King Alpin d. 834	79 Randver of Lethra 670	105 K. Alpin d. 834
	80 Sigurd Ring b. 730 AD	
	81 Ragnar Lothbrok	

Hebrews	Trojans / Scandinavians	Scythians / Milesians
Kings of Scotland:	Vikings in Ireland:	Kings of Scotland:
122 K. Kenneth I	82 Ivar the Boneless	106 K. Kenneth I d. 858
123 King Constantin I	83 Guthorm Ivarsson d. 890	107 King Constantin I
124 King Donald II	84 Ranald K. of Waterford	108 King Donald II
125 King Malcolm I	85 Ivar (Prince) of Waterford	109 King Malcolm I
126 King Kenneth II	86 Ivar II of Waterford d. 1000 AD	110 King Kenneth II
127 King Malcolm II	87 Ranald Ivarsson	111 King Malcolm II d. 1034
128 Bethoc	88 Ranald Ranaldsson	112 Bethoc
129 King Duncan I	89 Meargach MacRagnaill	113 King Duncan I
130 King Malcolm III	90 Solam	114 King Malcolm III
131 K. David I 1084-1153	91 Giolla Adhamnan b. 1065	115 K. David I 1084-1153
132 Prince Henry 1114-1152	92 Gillebride MacGille b. 1080	116 Prince Henry 1114-1152
133 Earl David 1152-1219	93 Somerled MacGillebride 1115	117 Earl David 1152-1219
134 Isobel of Huntingdon	94 Ranald MacSomhairle	118 Isobel of Huntingdon
135 Robert Bruce IV 1215-1295	95 Donald MacRaghnaill	119 Robert Bruce IV 1215-1295
136 Robert Bruce V 1243-1304	96 Angus Mor MacDonald	120 Robert Bruce V 1243-1304
137 K. Robert Bruce I 1274-1329	97 Angus Og MacDonald	121 K. Robert Bruce I 1274-1329
138 Marjorie Bruce 1296-1316 m. Walter Stewart III		122 Marjorie Bruce 1296-1316 m. Walter Stewart
139 Margaret Stewart m. John MacDonald	98 John (of Islay) MacDonald m. Princess Margaret Stewart	123 Margaret Stewart m. John MacDonald (#98)
140 John Mor Tanister MacDonald	99 John Mor Tanister McDonald	124 John Mor Tanister MacDonald
141 Donald MacDonald	100 Donald MacDonald	125 Donald MacDonald
142 John Mor MacDonald	101 John Mor MacDonald	126 John Mor MacDonald
143 John Cathanach MacDonald	102 John Cathanach MacDonald	127 John Cathanach MacDonald
144 Alex. Carragh MacDonald	103 Alex. Carragh MacDonald	128 Alex. Carragh MacDonald
145 Somhairle Buighe MacDonnel	104 Somhairle Buighe MacD	129 Somhairle Buighe MacD
146 James MacDonnell	105 James MacDonnell	130 James MacDonnell

Hebrews	Trojans / Scandinavians	Scythians / Milesians
147 Alex. Alasdair MacDonnell	106 Alex. Alasdair MacDonnell	131 Alex. Alasdair MacDonnell
148 James Archibald MacDonnell	107 James Archibald MacDonnell	132 James Archibald MacDonnell
149 Daniel MacDonnell	108 Daniel MacDonnell	133 Daniel MacDonnell
150 John MacDonnell	109 John MacDonnell	134 John MacDonnell
151 John Landon McDaniel Sr.	110 John Landon McDaniel Sr.	135 John Landon McDaniel
152 John McDaniel	111 John McDaniel	136 John McDaniel
153 John Ely McDonald (McDaniel)	112 John Ely McDonald (McDaniel)	137 John Ely McDonald (McDaniel)
154 Linville McDonald	113 Linville McDonald b 1768	138 Linville McDonald
155 Thomas McDonald	114 Thomas McDonald	139 Thomas McDonald
156 Rebecca Angeline McDonald	115 Rebecca Angeline McDonald	140 Rebecca Angeline McDonald
157 Rachel Eliza Banta	116 Rachel Eliza Banta	141 Rachel Eliza Banta
158 Minnie Evelyn Passmore	117 Minnie Evelyn Passmore	142 Minnie Evelyn Passmore
159 Leonard Jackson Stewart	118 Leonard Jackson Stewart	143 Leonard Jackson Stewart
160 Jan Eylander Jackson Stewart	119 Jan Eylander Jackson Stewart	144 Jan Eylander Jackson Stewart

Appendix 2 – The Hebrews

1 Adam Ben God
  b. 4000 BC d. 3070 BC
  m. Eve Bint God (co-equal)
2 Seth Ben Adam
  m. Azura Bint Adam (sister)
3 Enosh Ben Seth
  m. Noam Bint Seth (sister)
4 Cainan Ben Enos
  m. Mualeleth Bint Enosh
5 Mahalalel Ben Cainan
  m. Dinah Bint Barakiel
6 Jared Ben Mahalalel
  m. Baraka
7 Enoch Ben Jared
  m. Edna Bint Daniel
8 Methuselah Ben Enoch
  b. Edna Bint Azriel
9 Lamech Ben Methuselah
  m. Adah (Dawn)
10 Noah Ben Lamech
  m. Titea Emzara ggf: Methus.
	11 Shem Ben Noah
	  m. Sedegetelebab Bin Eliakim
	12 Arphaxad Ben Shem
	  m. Rasueja Bint Elam
	Cainan Ben Aphaxad
	  b. 2326 BC
	  m. Milka b. 2326 BC
	13 Shelah Ben Arphaxad
	  m. Muak Bint Kesed b. 2300
	14 Eber Ben Shelah
	  m. Azura Bint Cainan
	15 Peleg Ben Eber
	  m. Lamna
	16 Reu Ben Peleg
	  m. Ora
	17 Serug Ben Reu
	  m. ???
	18 Nahor Ben Serug
	  m. Iyosaka
	19 Terah Ben Nahor
	  m. Yawnu Bint Avram
		20 Abraham Ben Terah
		  b. 2053 BC in Ur
		  m. Sari Bint Haran
		21 Isaac Ben Abraham
		  m. Rebekah Bint Bethuel
		22 Jacob Israel Ben Isaac
		  m. Leah Bint Laban
		23 Judah Ben Jacob
		  m. Tamar Bint Epher
		24 Zara Zarah
		  m. Electra, dtr of Atlas,
		25 Darda Dardaius
		  m. Batea of Asia Illium Teucri

Appendix 3 – The Trojans

25 Darda Dardaius
   m. Batea of Asia Illium Teucri
26 Erichthonius Illium K
   of Arcadia
   m. Astyoche of Arcadia
27 Tros Acadia
   b. 1375 BC in Dardania
   m. Callirhoe
28 Ilus Troy
   m. Eurydice of Troy
29 Laomedon Troy
   m. Placia of Troy
30a Priam, High K. of Troy
   m. Hecuba of Phrygia
30b Tithonus of Troy
   b. 1304 BC d. 1237 BC
   m. Eos Aurora
31 Memnon Troy
   m. Troana, dtr of K. Priam
32 Tror (Thor)
   m. Sibil (Sif)
33 Loridi
   m. ???
34 Einridi
   m. ???
35 Vingethor b. 210 BC
   m. ???
36 Vingener
   m. ???

37 Moda
   m. ???
38 Magi
   m. ???
39 Sceaf (Seskef) (poss. Japheth
   bin Noe)
40 Bedwig
   b. 110 BC
41 Hwala King of Goths
   m. ???
42 Hathra (Athra)
   m. ???
43 Itermon or Itormann
   m. ???
44 Heremond
   b. 28 B.C. in Balikesir, Trkey
   d. Marmara, Balikesir, Trkey
   m. Sceaf, Queen of Troy
45 Sceldwa de Troy
   b. 5 B.C. in Yakutia, Russia
   d. A.D. 40 in Yakutia, Russia
46 Bedwa (Beaw), King of Troy
   b. 10 B.C. in Yakutia, Russia
   d. A.D. 45 in Yakutia, Russia
47 Taetwa Tecti
   b. 55 AD in Ghowr, Afghan
   d. 80 in Ghowr Afghanistan
   m. Lady Taetwa Tecti

48 Geata Jat Trojan
   b. A.D. 65 in Troy
   d. 155 in Ghowr, Afghanistan
   m. ???
49 Godwulf Trojan
   b. A.D. 80 in E. Europe
   d. 163 in Ghowr, Afghanistan
50 Flocwald of Asgard
   b. 100 in Asgard
   d. 179 in Maluku, Indonesia
51 Finn of Godwulf
   b. 130 in E. Europe
   d. 220 in Maluku, Indonesia
   m. ???
52 Frithuwulf
   b. 140
   (Freawine?)
53 Frealaf
   b. 165 in Asgaard, Asia
54 Fredwulf, Frithuwald, or Bor
   b. 190 in Asgard
   d. 245 in Picardie, France
   m. Freothalaf Trojan 215-260
   m. Beltsa Asgard 215-???
55 Odin

Appendix 4 – The Scandinavians

55 Odin (Woden, Wuotan)	64 Domar Domaldasson	75 Eystein Adilsson
b. 215 in Asgard, or E. Europ	b. 361	b. 594 Vaermland, Sweden
d. 300 in Lake Malar, Upps.	m. Droft Danspsdotter b. 365	76 Yngvar (The Tall)
m. Frigg Cadwalladatter	65 Dyggvi I Domarsson	Eysteinsson
b. 223 in Asgaard, Trkstn	b. 382 Sweden	b. 616 Sweden
56 Yngvi Tyrkja	66 Dag "the Wise" Dyggvasson	d. Sten, Esthland
m. Friege Fren	b. 403 in Sweden	77 Skira Ingvarsson
57 Njord Odinsson K. of	67 Agni Dagsson	b. 620
Swedes	b. 424 Sweden	78 Radbard K. of Gardgarige
b. 214 Noatun, Sweden	d. Agnefit, Stockholm	b. 638 Russia
m. sister-wife Sviergedottir	68 Alrek Agnasson	m. Aud Ivarsdottir,
m. Skadi Thjazisdottir (Giant)	b. 445 in Noatun, Sweden	b. 643 in Am, Denmark
58 Yngvi Frey, King of Uppsala	69 Yngvi Alreksson	79 Randver of Lethra
b. 242 Uppsala	b. 466 Sweden	b. 670 Denmark,
m. Gerd Gymersdotter b 239	70 Jorund Yngvasson	m. Ingild Unknown, b. 675
59 Fjolnir Yngvi Freysson	b. 487 Sweden	80 Sigurd Ring
b. 256 Uppsala	d. Oddesund, Jutland, Denm	King of Sweden
d. ____ Hleithra, Denmark	71 Aun (The Aged) Ani	b. 730 Sweden, d. 812 Denm.
60 Svegdi Fjolnarsson	b. 509 Upsala	m. Alfhild Gandolfsdottir
b. 281 Uppsala	72 Egil Aunsson	81 Ragnar Lodbrok
m. Vana Svitjod b. 281	b. about 530	K. of Denmark
61 Vanlandi Svegdasson	73 Ottar (Vendilkraka) Egilsson	b. 760, Uppsala
b. 298 Sweden	b. 551 Upsala	d. Northumbria
m. Driva Snaersdotter b. 302	d. 572 Limfjord Denmark	
62 Visbur Vanlandasson	74 Adilis "Athils" Ottarsson	
b. 319 Swden	b. 572 Upsala	
m Authisdottir b. 323	m. Yrsa Helgasdatter	
63 Domaldi Visbursson	b. 565 Denmark	
b. 340 Sweden		

Appendix 5 – The Scythians

10 Noah Ben Lamech 　m. Titea Emzara 11 Japheth 12 Magog, progenitor of 　Scythians 　b Jobath c Fathochta 13 a Baoth 2500 – d. Scythia 　m. Feninsa Farsa (Celtic tradition inserts fifteen generations here: Hisrau, Ezra, Ra, Aber, Aoth, Ethec, Aurthack, Ecthactus, Mair, Simeon, Boibus, Thoi, Ogomuin, Fethuir, Lamfind)	14 Fenius Farsaidh 2533-1800?? 　K. of Scythia 　(See Appendix, Seneschals) 15 Niul Nemnach, K. Scythia 　b. 2401 in Eathena 16 Gaodhal Glas 2305-2246 Egy. 17 Asruth 2280-2196 b. Egypt 18 Sruth 2240 – 2121 (?) b. Egpt 19 Eimher (Heber Scutt) 2373 – 20 Beoman 2265- 21 Oghaman, K of Scythia 　2235-1736 (?) 22 Tait, King of Scythia 2230- 23 Agnon 2003-1960	24 Lamhfionn Pr. of Scythia 25 Eimhir Glunfionn 2213- 26 Agnan Fionn 2180 – 27 Faobhar (Febric Glas) 2133 28 Nenuall 1899- 29 Nuadhad 1880- 30 Ealloid (Alladh) 1855- 31 Earchada (Arcadh) 1830-? 32 Deaghata 1800- ? 33 Brath 1805-1715 34 Breoghan 1799-1680 35 Bile d. 1739 36 Milesius 1853-1806 37 Heremon 　m. Queen Tea Tephi, Ireland

Appendix 6 – The Lineage of Queen Tea Tephi

33 David 1st King of Judah 　m. Bathsheba bat Ammiel 34 Solomon ben David 2nd K 　m. Naamah Pr. Of Ammon 35 Rehoboam 3rd K of Israel 　m. Macaah of Gosher 36 Abija 4th K of Judah 　m. Ana bat Ahimaaz 37 Asa 5th K of Judah 　m. Azubah 38 Jehoshapat 6th K of Judah 　m. dtr of Omri the Wicked 39 Jehoram 7th K of Judah 　m. Athalia dtr of Jezebel 　　& Ahab K. of Israel	40 Ozias 8th King of Judah 　m. Zibiah of Beersheba (Queen Athaliah reigned as 9th) 41 Josiah 10th K of Judah 　m. Jehoaddin of Jerusalem 42 Amaziah 11th K of Judah 　m. Jecoliah of Jerusalem 43 Uzziah 12th K of Judah 　m. Jerusha, High Priestess 　　of Israel 44 Joatham 13th K of Judah 　m. Ahio bat Azrikam 45 Achaz 14th K of Judah 　m. Abijah bat Zechariah	46 Ezechias 15th King of Judah 　m. Hephzibah bat Isaiah 47 Manasses 16th K of Judah 　m. Meshullemeth bat Haruz 48 Amon 17th K of Judah 　m. Jedidah of Bozkath 49 Josiah 18th K of Judah 　m. Zebidah of Rumah 50 Johanan (Cr. Pr.) of Judah 　m. ??? 51 Tamar bat Johanan 　m. Lugaid mac Itha 52 Tea Tephi 　m. Heremon #37

Appendix 7 – The Irish

O'Hart, Irish Pedigrees	O'Hart	O'Hart
Queen Tea Tephi	60 Cobhthach Coalbreag	80 K. Tuathal Teachtmar
m. #37 King Heremon	r. 591-451 BC	b. 056 AD
38 Irial Faidh	61 Meilage	m. Baine Sgaile
39 Eithriall	62 Jaran Gleofathach	81 Felim Rachtmar b. 80
40 Follain	63 Coula Cruaidh Cealgach	m. Ughna Olichrothach
41 Tighernmas d. 1543 BC	64 Oiliolla Caisfhiachach	Denmark
42 Eanbotha	65 Eochaidh Foltleathan	82 Conn Ceadchathach
43 Smiorguil	66 Aongus Tuirmheach	(of the 100 Battles)
44 Fiachadh Labhri	(Teamharch 384-324 BC)	m. Landabaria of Ireland
45 Aongus Ollmuch	67 Eana Aighneach	83 Art Ean Flier
46 Maoin	r. 312-292 BC	m. Maedhbh Connan
47 Rotheachta	68 Labhra Suire	m. Achtan Acha
48 Dein	69 Blathucha	84 Cormac Ulfada
49 Siorna Saoghalach	70 Easamhuin Famhua	m. Eithne Ollamhdfha
50 Oliolla Olchaoin	71 Roighnein Ruadh	85 Caibre Liffeachair
51 Giallchadh d. 787 BC	72 Fionnlaoch	d. 284 AD
52 Nuadhas FionnFail	73 Fian	86 Fiachadh Sreabthuine
53 Aodhain Glas	74 Eochaidh Feidhlioch	87 Muireadhach Tireach
54 Simeon Breac	r. 142-130 BC	88 Eochaidh Moigmeodhin
55 Muirteadach Bolgrach	75 Freas Nar-Lothar	89 Nail of the 9 Hostages =101
56 Fiachadh Toigrach	76 Lughaidh Raidhdearg	90 Eogan
57 Duach Laidhrach	77 Criomhthan Niadhnar r. 7-9 AD	91 K. Murireadhach
58 Eochaidh Bualgllerg	78 Fearaidhach Feachtnuigh	(Earca?)
59 Ugaine More the Great	79 Fiachadh Fionoluidh	92 Erc

Appendix 8 – The Kings of Ancient Ireland / Scotland

The Viking Kings of Ireland	The Kings of Argyll in Scotland
(from #81 Ragnar Lothbrok)	(from #37 Heremon)
82 Ivar the Boneless	93 King Fergus More d. 501
m. Ingiald Ragnarsdottir	94 King Dongard
83 Guthorm Ivarsson	95 King Conran
d. 890	96 King Aidan
K. of Dublin	97 King Eugene IV
84 Ranald K. of Waterford	98 King Donald IV
d 921	99 Dongard
85 Ivar (Prince) of Waterford	100 King Eugene V
of the Isle of Man	101 Findan
86 Ivar II of Waterford d. 1000	102 King Eugene VII
87 Ranald Ivarsson	103 King Etfinus
b. 974 Dublin	104 King Achaius
88 Ranald Ranaldsson	105 King Alpin d. 834
b. Perth, Scotland	
89 Meargach MacRagnaill	Kings of Scotland
b. 1010 Dublin	106 King Kenneth I
90 Solam	107 King Constantin I
b. Dublin	108 King Donald II
91 Giolla Adhamnan	109 King Malcolm I
b. 1065 Scotland	110 King Kenneth II
92 Gillebride MacGille Adomnan	111 King Malcolm II
b. 1085 Ireland	112 Bethoc
93 Somerled MacGillebride	m. Bishop Crinan
b. 1115 Scotland d. 1164	113 King Duncan I
	m. Sybil
	114 King Malcolm III
	m. Margaret of Wessex

Appendix 9 – The Donalds / McDonalds

The Scots / Donalds	The McDonalds	The Americans
93 Somerled MacGillebride	100 Donald MacDonald	109 John MacDonnell
b. 1115 Scotland d. 1164	b. 1407 Scotland	b. 1670 Ireland
94 Ranald MacSomhairle	101 John Mor MacDonald	d. killed by Indians in Virginia
b. 1153 Scotland d. 1207	b. 1445 Ireland	m. Susannah Carrington
(Brother of Angus, d. 1210)	m. Sabina O'Neill	m. Joan Lloyd
(See Stewart ancestry)	102 John Cathanach MacD	110 John Landon McDaniel Sr.
m. Fonia	B. 1435 Ireland	b. 1695 Virginia
95 Donald MacRaghnaill	103 Alexander Carragh MacD	111 John McDaniel
b. 1200 Scotland d. 1250	b. 1478 Ireland (Ulster)	b. 1720 Virginia
m. NN dtr of Walter Stewart	104 Somhairle Buidhe MacD	112 John Ely McDonald (McDaniel)
96 Angus Mor MacDonald	b. 1505 Ireland	b. 1740, Virginia
b. 1248 Scotland d. 1292	105 James MacDonnell	113 Linville McDonald
97 Angus Og MacDonald	b. 1550 (d. Ireland)	b. 1768 North Carolina
b. 1274 Scotland d. 1329	106 Alexander Alasdair	114 Thomas McDonald
98 John (of Islay) MacDonald	MacDonnell	b. 1803 North Carolina
b. 1318 Scotland	b. 1580 (d. Ireland)	115 Rebecca Angeline McDonald
m. Princess Margaret Stewart	107 James Archibald MacD	b. 1842 Illinois
99 John Mor Tanister MacD	b. 1615 Ireland	m. John Walter Banta
b. 1360 Scotland	m. Mary O'Brien	116 Rachel Eliza Banta
	108 Daniel MacDonnell	m. Leonard J. Passmore
	b. 1640 Antrim, Ireland	117 Minnie Evelyn Passmore
	m. Penelope O'Byrne	m. Alva Clinton Stewart
		118 Leonard Jackson Stewart
		m. Faye Marilyn Milor
		119 Jan Eylander Jackson Stewart
		m. Misa Abe

Bibliography

Bryant, Jacob (1774). *A New System or an Analysis of Ancient Mythology*, Wherein an Attempt is made to divest Tradition of Fable; and to reduce the Truth to its Original Purity. London: T. Payne, P. Elmsly, B. White, J. Walter (MDCCLXXIV).

Carey, John (1990), "The Ancestry of Fenius Farsaid."
Celtica: Journal of the School of Celtic Studies, 21, 104-112.
http : // www.celt.dias.ie/

Haigh, Daniel Henry (1861). *The Conquest of Britain by the Saxons*: A Harmony of the "Historia Britonum", the Writings of Gildas, the "Brut," and the Saxon Chronicle, With Reference to the Events of the Fifth and Sixth Centuries. London: J.R. Smith.

Jaski, Bart. "Aeneas and Fenius: a classical case of mistaken identity."
https://www.academia.edu / es/1273936/Aeneas_and_Fenius_a_classical_case_of_mistaken_identity.

Nanni, Giovanni (1432-1501). *An Historical Treatise of the Travels of Noah into Europe:* Containing the first inhabitation and peopling thereof. Transl. Richard Lynche. London: Adam Islip, 1601.

Monachus, Theodoricus, "An Account of the Ancient History of the Norwegian Kings," Translated and annotated by David and Ian McDougall (1998). Viking Society for Northern Research: University College London.

Milner, W.M.H. (1902). *The Royal House of Britain: An Enduring Dynasty.* Covenant Publishers, 12th Revised Edition, 1952.

O'Hart, John (1876). *Irish Pedigrees: The Origin and Stem of the Irish Nation* (5th Edition). Genealogical Publishing Co., 1999.

Utley, Francis Lee, 1941. "The One Hundred Three Names of Noah's Wife."
Speculum, Vol. 16, No. 4 (Oct. 1941) pp. 426-452.

www.ingramcontent.com/pod-product-compliance
Lightning Source LLC
Chambersburg PA
CBHW081350160426
43197CB00015B/2719